Do It Well.
Make It Fun.

Do It Well.
Well.
Make It Fun.

The Key *to* Success *in* Life, Death,
and Almost Everything *in* Between

Ronald P. Culberson

GREENLEAF
BOOK GROUP PRESS

Published by Greenleaf Book Group Press
Austin, Texas
www.gbgpress.com

Distributed by Greenleaf Book Group LLC

For ordering information or special discounts for bulk purchases, please contact Greenleaf Book Group LLC at PO Box 91869, Austin, TX 78709, 512.891.6100.

Design and composition by Greenleaf Book Group LLC
Cover design by Greenleaf Book Group LLC

Publisher's Cataloging-In-Publication Data
(Prepared by The Donohue Group, Inc.)
Culberson, Ron.
   Do it well. Make it fun. : the key to success in life, death, and almost everything in between / Ron Culberson. — 1st ed.
   p. ; cm.
   Includes bibliographical references and index.
   ISBN: 978-1-60832-285-5
   1. Success. 2. Life—Humor. 3. Work-life balance. 4. Wit and humor—Psychological aspects. 5. Excellence. I. Title.
BJ1611 .C85 2012
158.1   2011944700

Part of the Tree Neutral® program, which offsets the number of trees consumed in the production and printing of this book by taking proactive steps, such as planting trees in direct proportion to the number of trees used: www.treeneutral.com

Printed in the United States of America on acid-free paper

12 13 14 15 16   10 9 8 7 6 5 4 3 2 1

First Edition

To my parents and siblings, who demonstrated excellent values and always laughed at me (in a good way).

CONTENTS

Section 3: All Work and No Play Is, Well, Work

Acknowledgments

Publishing a book requires much more than writing words on a page—the writing part is hard enough. The book you have in your hand is the result of a team effort. Of course, I am the most important member of the team so I'll begin by acknowledging all the hard work that I did. In addition to me . . .

My wife Wendy and my kids Ryan and Caitlin have always been supportive of my unusual career and they're the ones who put up with my self doubt and overcompensation when I'm not sure what I'm doing. They're amateur psychologists of the highest order.

My mastermind group of Laura, Waldo, Simon, Stephen, Tim, Chad, Marty, Ruby, and Colette encouraged me to go down this Do it Well. Make it Fun. path. So if it ends badly, I will most certainly blame them.

Ed Ugel is a gifted writer and offered to review a few early chapters in the book. His simple response made a huge difference to me. He said, "I'm so glad you can actually write."

Theo Androus suggested that my concept of Do it Well. Make it Fun. was "money." He'll be paying the bills in the event of any short-falls.

David Jordan Haas has been an incredible friend and supporter of my work. He's either very kind and generous, or he's mentally imbal-anced. I believe it's the former.

A number of colleagues and friends are mentioned in this book. Those mentions should be acknowledgment enough, don't you think?

And finally, my thanks to the folks at Greenleaf Book Group. Clint is a friend and a great businessman. He, Justin, and Bill helped me conceptualize this book. Then Natalie, Andrea, Jenn, Kris, Jeanne, Jay, and Neil kept me on track throughout the process.

I am grateful for most things in my life and, more importantly, for the people in my life.

There is no labor a person does that is undignified, if they do it right.

—Bill Cosby

Introduction

How many personal development books are on your bookshelf?

If there are none, good for you. Clearly, you're unaware of your many faults and the need for self improvement. You could use this book. It might just help you. But probably not.

If you have several hundred personal development books on your shelf, you have a personal development addiction problem.

You're probably familiar with all the promises made by famous self-help books such as *The 7 Habits of Highly Effective Nuns* or *The 6 Steps to the Top of Your Stairs*. They give you tangible numerical promises to turn your miserable existence into success, wealth, and buns of steel.

This book only has only two steps (Do it well. Make it fun.) and one promise (Success). The concept is so simple. Do things well, make them fun, and you'll find more success in your life. Because of its simplicity, this concept will make every other personal development book obsolete. At least that's what I said to my publisher.

In fact, I'm thinking that you should destroy all of your other personal development books right now. Because you will never need them again . . . now that you own a copy of *Do It Well. Make It Fun.* At least I hope you own it. If you borrowed it or checked it out of the library, I'd be very disappointed. Can't you at least invest a few dollars in your success?

Seriously, why is this book so valuable? Because it contradicts years of brainwashing by earnest psychologists, new age gurus, and overexposed Oprahs. It offers a simple process to address everything in your life from boring meetings at work to dull relationships at home. It covers stress, health, communication, parenting, conflict, meetings, hobbies, and even death (in a pre-death kind of way). Let's just say it has a lot of good ideas boiled down to one simple concept —**Do it well. Make it fun**.

So why do *you* need this book? Good question. Let me explain by taking you on a short regressive journey. Go back with me to your childhood. Not all the way back to the traumatic womb-to-world experience, or to the time when you realized your parents never really loved you. I'm not concerned about that and, quite honestly, you need to stop caring about that as well. Instead, go back to those times as a child when we laughed in school, snickered at the dinner table, or God forbid, laughed out loud during church (or equally devastating location for you nonchurchgoing readers). Do you remember what we were told? Do you remember how it felt to hear, "That's not funny" from an overbearing and terminally serious adult? Do you remember how older people tried to beat us down just for being jovial?

It was more devastating than you think.

All those times we were told to "act your age," "grow up," or "wipe that smile off your face," we were basically belittled for embracing the fun side of life. We were ridiculed for catching a simple ray of light. We were scorned for wanting to relish the joy of the moment. And as a result, we believed the myth that successful, responsible, and respectable adults should be deeply and perpetually serious.

What a load of crap. I get verklempt just thinking about the millions of people who fell prey to this myth. Those who, as adults, cannot enjoy a *Far Side* cartoon, an episode of *Seinfeld*, or the cleansing sound of a whoopee cushion. They are lost souls trapped in a world void of balance who will one day be diagnosed as dead men walking, living their remaining days in an assisted-laughing facility.

It's this mistaken pursuit of seriousness that drove us away from fun and humor. But the pursuit of seriousness, ironically, also drove us away from excellence—for we were led to believe that seriousness was all that was needed to tackle this big cruel world. And that led to a lack of excellence and to a life of mediocrity, or what the bell curve refers to as average.

Do you really want average to be your goal? I don't. I wouldn't want an average car mechanic. I wouldn't want to eat in an average restaurant. And I certainly wouldn't want an average cardiovascular surgeon, although I'd accept an average-*looking* surgeon with above-average skills. And yet most of us settle for average every single day when we could achieve so much more with a little more focus, a little more effort, and a little more, uh, more.

Someone, probably a mediocre motivational speaker, once said, "The only difference between try and triumph is a little umph." Yes, it's cliché, but you get the point. The key to success is excellence, not seriousness. We will never make it on seriousness alone. We need to strive for excellence in every aspect of our life.

Abraham Lincoln, who I believe influenced the development of the luxury car, once said, "It's not about the days in your life, but the life in your days."

He was addressing a state of mind and a manner of existence. It's about the value with which we live rather than the amount of time we have left. When we focus on value, we achieve a higher level of richness and success in our lives.

That's the essence of this book.

Do it well. Make it fun.

Focus on excellence *and* joy.

Add life to our days. It's truly that simple.

Chapter 1

Seriously, Take Life Fun Day at a Time (or A Bit More of the Introduction That Would Have Made the Introduction Chapter Too Long)

On September 9, 2009, I headed south for a four-day motorcycle trip with my brother, his brother-in-law, and his nephew. It was a beautiful day, but a storm was heading my way. I was just north of Roanoke, Virginia, where I was going to hunker down in a Starbucks until the storm passed over. I was riding carefree, or as carefree as a 48-year-old man with hemorrhoids can (I know, TMI), on my Harley Davidson 1200 Custom Sportster. I was going about 60 mph (the legal speed limit, by the way) on a four-lane divided highway, and before I realized what was happening, a man made an uninsured left turn right in front of me.

My first reaction was, "Dang it, this is a new helmet."

My second reaction was, "Dang it, I'm only 48."

My third and last reaction was to do exactly what I was taught in my motorcycle safety class—lock both brakes and slide in a straight line around the danger. I slid around the front end of the truck onto a narrow, three-foot-wide shoulder of grass and gravel. Then, I hit a large patch of gravel, and my bike slid out from under me.

At this point, I blacked out. I have since learned that blacking out is normal when our brains want to hide from the scary potential of what might be happening. I awoke a second or two later to the sound of something dragging through the gravel. Turns out, that something was my mouth.

I suspected that my mouth dragging through gravel wasn't good. I thought for sure my front teeth would be gone.

Once I came to a stop, I stood up and surveyed the damage. I looked down at my body and everything was still attached. That was good. I looked at my bike and one side was all smashed up. That wasn't so good, but it was sure better than one side of me being smashed up. Then, I ran over to the one good mirror left on my bike to get a look at my face. My teeth were all there but I had a huge gash across my chin and from my cheekbones down to my jaw, my face was all cut up. It was a bloody, gnarly mess. But I was alive. And from all I could tell, I was in pretty decent shape. Nonetheless, I knew that the next few hours would be very stressful.

I remember making a conscious decision to make the best of the situation and to see if I could find even the slightest bit of humor over the next few hours.

The first thing I noticed was that my mangled motorcycle had landed in front of a towing company. Bonus! That was one way to get around the lack of towing coverage in my insurance policy.

The next thing I noticed was that an EMT, an emergency medical technician, was standing in the driveway of the towing company when the accident happened. How lucky was that? I had medical help right there.

The EMT rushed over to me, got right up in my face, and said, "What day is it?"

I couldn't help but laugh.

I understood the purpose of his question. He was trying to determine if I had experienced head trauma. But given the circumstances, that I was walking around and mostly concerned about the potential damage to my professional-speaker face, I thought the question was funny. So, I looked back at him and said, "Dude, look at me. My bloody face doesn't really care if it's Wednesday or Thursday!"

He didn't appreciate the sarcasm. And because I couldn't tell him the date quickly enough, he made me lie down on the ground until the ambulance arrived. I was just happy that any head trauma I had didn't affect my ability to appreciate irony.

The ambulance pulled up about twenty minutes later and the *real* EMTs strapped me onto a backboard and put a neck brace on me as a precaution for possible neck or back injury. Then they sped to the hospital. Well, *sped* might be a slight exaggeration. In reality, they went below the speed limit without lights or sirens and stopped for a Slurpee at 7-11 on the way. I was a little disappointed but reassured that my condition was not critical.

When I got to the ER, the attending physician came into the exam room and said, "How are you doing?"

It seemed like such an odd question. I was in an emergency room after having a motorcycle accident. How was I supposed to be doing?

So, I said, "Well, I finally appreciate the significance of my father's repeated admonition to keep my chin up."

"Yep, right-o," he said.

Then he left.

I was offended by his total lack of appreciation for a perfectly delivered bit of humor. Here, a patient with a mangled face offered witty repartee and he didn't even respond. That's when I realized I had my work cut out for me if I was going to survive the overzealous seriousness of a hospital setting.

After the X-rays revealed no broken bones or embedded gravel, the nurse needed to clean up my face before the physician's assistant stitched up my chin. She was busy scrubbing my chin with sterile saline and what appeared to be 40-grit sandpaper when I said to her, "After the facial, do you think I could get a cucumber wrap and a pedicure?"

She burst out laughing, and from that point on, we were bedside buddies. At one point, I even caught her admiring my Mickey Mouse tattoo. At 48, I had almost forgotten what it was like for an attractive woman to admire my tattoo. The gash in my chin almost sewed itself up.

Two days after my motorcycle accident, I went to see my family doctor, Dr. Lee. My face was a scabby, oozing mess, not unlike the appearance of apple crisp but without the deliciousness. Dr. Lee said my chin was healing nicely, but she told me that I needed to get the stitches out before I left town for a series of speaking engagements the following week. She wanted me to come in first thing on Monday morning. The problem was, I had an 8:00 a.m. flight to Texas that day. Dr. Lee said I had to change the flight because the stitches *"must* come out" sooner rather than later.

I called my travel agent, Jan, and was shocked to discover that the airline's fee to change my flight from 8:00 a.m. to 1:00 p.m. was $1,000. It still baffles me that moving my seat from one flight to another costs the airline that much money. It's not like they had to restock the galley and bring in a new crew because I was now on a new flight. I *do* consume a lot of coffee when I fly—but not quite $1,000 worth.

Discouraged by this fee, I complained to my travel agent about United Airlines, the airline industry, the travel industry, and that obnoxious left-turn-impaired, uninsured driver that put me in this position in the first place.

Jan couldn't fix the fee but she did offer one simple, and ultimately wise, piece of advice. She said, "Go to the United counter at the airport and let the ticket agent see your face. When you request a change in flights, she won't have the heart to charge you $1,000."

That's why I love Jan. She knows how to work the system.

I went straight to the airport, walked up to the United ticket counter, where two agents were working, and with a very serious expression on my face, I pointed to my scabby, stitched-up chin and said, "I got this from turbulence on my last flight and I'd like to request a refund."

Both women went pale. They stared at me as if they had found heroin and a pipe bomb in my carry-on bag.

Savoring the moment, I let them squirm for a few seconds before saying, "Nah, just kidding. I had a motorcycle accident and need to change a flight. But the United agent on the phone said I had to pay $1,000. That seems like a lot considering what I've been through. Can you help me?"

One of the women dove for her keyboard and started typing furiously.

"I can fix that," she said.

A few minutes later, I left the airport with a new ticket for a fee of only $75.

My face was a mess and I still had ten stitches. But I had conquered two challenges. An uninsured driver ... and a unhelpful United phone rep.

In my humble opinion, I did that pretty well and had a lot of fun.

So, what's my point? I think this entire experience was a perfect example of the powerful combination of doing things well and making them fun.

I used my motorcycle skills to avoid death or dismemberment. Then I made the unpleasant experience of visiting the ER as fun as it possibly could be. I managed to accomplish the same thing when I dealt with the ticket agents. I did everything as well as I could while making the process as fun as I could.

Did it well. Made it fun. Bought the T-shirt.

In this book, I will be showing you how to do this with your everyday experiences so that when you encounter your own uninsured driver or an overly serious ER physician, you can respond in a healthy, fun, and life-enriching way.

In order to do this, we have to look at everything we do as a process that involves a series of steps. When we got out of bed this morning, we engaged in a process: Alarm goes off, we grumble, we hit the snooze button, we grumble, alarm goes off again, we turn off the alarm, we get out of bed, we grumble, we get back in bed, we get out of bed, etc. Every experience in life can be broken down into steps like this. Then, every step in every experience has the potential of being improved *and* being more fun. Remember, we're striving for better than average. Once we add the two concepts together, we can be a well of fun. See how I did that? I know, it's a gift.

As a hospice social worker I saw people handle the most serious situations that we'll ever experience with grace and dignity. As a professional humorist, I have witnessed some of the most hilarious situations we'll ever experience. Personal success in every arena of our lives is a result of combining the two. I believe it is THE secret to life.

That's why you can get rid of all the other personal development books. If you're willing to do it well and make it fun, you won't need them.

So let's start this journey with a close look at the value of this very moment, because if you miss it, it will be over before you know it.

Section 1:

It's All About Me, Myself, and I

Chapter 2

NOW You're Onto Something

Thanksgiving in my family involves gorging ourselves on turkey, stuffing, mashed potatoes, that green bean casserole with the fake onion rings on top, and canned, gelatinous cranberry sauce that's been mashed up with a fork so we don't see the shape of the can on it. We eat way more than we want, more than we need, and we talk more than we should. Inevitably, the conversation moves beyond an update on everyone's perfect children to an I-can-one-up-you story fest about the funny, embarrassing, and, I suspect, often manufactured events from our past.

Why is it that we can remember word for word what our mother said to us when the dog ate her shoe but we can't remember where we left our car keys?

It's because we love to relive the past.

We love to talk about it, idolize it, embellish it, and compare it to all that is not right with the world today. We discuss it as if, by doing so, it will come back more gloriously than the inaccurate way we remember it. But, and I hate to break this to you, the past is gone. It won't be back.

I'm fascinated by the way older adults can talk for hours about the past but seem to have little or no interest in the present—especially when it comes to repeating a story they told us seven minutes earlier. To them, contemporary television and pop music are garbage compared to the masterpieces of the past. Facebook and Twitter are incomprehensible forms of communication that involve some sort of voodoo. And the values displayed by young people are akin to those of Satan.

Younger adults, on the other hand, are mostly concerned about the future. They're thinking about their next job or how much money they'll make or where they'll live. They can't wait until their ship comes in and they've achieved a prosperous and successful life.

The common thread between these two groups of people is that neither focuses on the present. And this holds true throughout much of our lives. We reminisce about, and in some cases regret, the past, or we look with anticipation of, and in some cases worry about, the future. And all the while, the present is right here wanting to be noticed.

NOW Is Where It's At

In his phenomenal bestseller, *The Power of Now*, Eckhart Tolle emphasizes the importance of focusing on the here and now. Essentially, Tolle suggests that most stress in our lives comes from being *here* (whatever we're experiencing in the present moment) and wanting to be *there* (doing anything better, more exciting, or more fulfilling than the present moment). In other words, we fill our present state of mind with fantasies of the future or memories of the past. Instead of, he points out, focusing on the present, which is the only thing we can truly control.

Tolle's book had a huge impact on me because it forced me to see the error in my thinking. I tend to live in my head, often obsessing about something I wish I had done, or not done, in the past or getting nervous about something I have to do in the future. I'm either beating myself up for all the marketing calls I didn't make last week or worrying about whether the audience will like a new story. In the process of these obsessions, I'm missing the present moment, which right now includes a funky squirrel sunbathing on my deck (seriously, there's a squirrel stretched out on the rail of my deck) or a conversation I could have with a friend who is ill—that is, if I wasn't worrying about the calls and the story. Ironically, many times, I can eliminate my worries by doing something right now. Instead, many of us (and by "us" I mean me) choose to remain in our heads rather than focus on what we can do or appreciate right now.

The essence of doing it well and making it fun lies in the moment. Whenever we're doing an activity or working on a project, we have the opportunity to focus intently on making the process better and more enjoyable.

As you'll see throughout this book, my goal is to simplify the principles in life so we can implement them more easily with as few steps as possible. The simplified principle or process for focusing on the present is as follows:

Feel an Emotion ➤ Ignore the Invalid Thoughts ➤ Take Action

Let's see how it works. When we feel pressure at work or stress at home, often as a nagging sensation in our gut, if it's not due to kidney stones or a bad burrito, the feeling or tension is usually due to the thoughts we are thinking rather than what's really happening in the external world. For instance, if I have a column due tomorrow (which I do) and I have not yet begun it (which I have not), then most likely my thoughts are going wild (which they are) with the infinite possibilities of what might happen if I don't get the column done. Add to this the little voices in my head that tell me I'm an idiot for putting off the writing, I'm not really a good writer, and I could have written this column earlier, and I begin to work myself into a frenzy. In other words, my stress is not inherently caused by the column that's due but by my beliefs about myself and what might happen if the column doesn't get done. This leads to wasted time spent on the beliefs rather than the action needed to address the issue in the first place—writing the column.

If we could channel all of that emotional energy into focusing on the project at hand, we could shift our focus to the here and now. I can't change what will happen, and I can't alter the fact that I put the column off so long. But I'm *not* an idiot and I can change what I do right now. And right now, I need to be working on the blessed column. So, if you'll pardon me, I'm going to work on my column and get back to this chapter tomorrow.

Mary Got It

Over the past few years, I've had a recurring near-death experience. I didn't see a tunnel or a light, and I didn't meet Shirley MacLaine. But I did miss an opportunity to reach out to several people who were ill and eventually died.

Here's what happened. I became aware of friends and acquaintances in my church or my community who were ill and I promptly put a note on my to-do list to send them a card or give them a call. But, due to the fact that my to-do list is never too-done, I kept putting off the cards and the calls. In every case (a total of five), the person died before I contacted them. In some cases, I did not realize how sick the person was. In others, I just put it off because, in my mind, I imagined that there was always more time. I shared this with a friend who told me that no matter how sick he became, he never wanted me to put his name on my to-do list. Good call.

The founder of Send Out Cards, Kody Bateman started his company for this very reason. He failed to connect with his brother over a period of several months and then his brother died in an accident. So Kody created a company to encourage people to reach out to others.

He realized the power of the right-now connection and the value of greeting cards to make that connection.

One of the most extraordinary "now" experiences I ever had was featured in my first book, *Is Your Glass Laugh Full?* Because it's so relevant to this topic, I'll share it again here.

In the fall of 1987, I was in my second year as a hospice home care social worker. As a member of an interdisciplinary team of health care professionals, I was expected to attend to the psychosocial concerns of people who were terminally ill and to be a source for support to their families.

On a beautiful October day, I arrived at the home of Mary Burton (not her real name), a 68-year-old wife and mother of three. Mary had been married to her husband, Joe, for nearly 50 years. Her three daughters were grown and each had a family and a successful career. Mary was a loving parent and was the major reason for her family's success. Mary was also dying of cancer and had been given less than six months to live. As I arrived at Mary's house that day, I had no idea she would teach me one of the greatest lessons I would ever learn.

Joe welcomed me at the door and politely escorted me into Mary's bedroom. He then excused himself so Mary and I could get better acquainted. Mary was neatly perched on her bed, anxiously awaiting her afternoon "visitor." Her face lit up as I entered the room and she invited me to sit down and make myself comfortable. It did not take long for me to understand why Mary was the love of her family.

As I sat in her room that day, I saw firsthand the significant role she played in her family's life. She loved her husband and cared for him as if he were breakable. She did this, not in a smothering way, but the way you treasure something valuable. She loved her children, and while she gave of herself freely to them, it was clear she had also provided firm yet understanding discipline. I recognized this by the way in which she and her family showed so much respect and courtesy to me *and* to each other. She spoke fondly of her life and expressed satisfaction in the way it all "turned out." At the same time, she expressed sincere respect for her illness and hoped her current state of relative well-being would last so she could savor the time with her loved ones. After about 45 minutes of conversation, I asked to talk with Joe and the one daughter, Jill, who was there at the time of my visit. They shared their sense of grief at the thought of losing Mary and yet they showed a strength that clearly came from her.

I left Mary's house that day feeling confident that she and her family would get through this difficult experience as we are all supposed to—by leaning on the shoulders of those we love. And since Mary was doing rather well, despite her illness, I looked forward to her family using the next few months to build upon their already strong relationships.

Two weeks after my visit, Mary was admitted to the Hospice of Northern Virginia's inpatient unit, a unit reserved for patients in crisis or near death. Apparently, she had taken a dramatic turn for the worse during the previous two days, but her doctors felt it was something treatable and not related to her cancer. They wanted to monitor her for a few days and then get her back home.

The moment I walked into Mary's hospice room, I saw how dramatic the change in her condition was. The color in her face was gone. She was having trouble breathing. And her listless body sank into the mattress as though she had no strength.

As I approached, a comforting look of recognition warmed her face. I took her frail hand in mine and asked, "How are you doing?"

"Not good," she whispered.

"Are you getting what you need?"

"They're spoiling me," she said with a weak grin. "The nurses have been so nice—they seem to anticipate my every need."

Then Mary rose up on her elbows, took a long look around the room and announced, "This place is beautiful. I had heard so much about it, *I was dying to see it!*" I froze, not knowing how to respond.

Mary closed her eyes, fell back on her pillow, and let loose a weak burst of laughter.

"Can you believe I said that?" she asked, shaking her head in disbelief.

We laughed together while I marveled at her brave use of humor in the face of such daunting circumstances.

Six hours later, Mary died.

Mary valued the power of the now. She realized the severity of her situation but was not willing to trade that in and risk missing a rich moment of laughter. That's what I'm talking about.

So, how can we make your present moments better and more fun?

* * * *

In each of the chapters in this book, I will offer some simple steps to achieve Do It Well, Make It Fun success. I call these my Well-Fun Tips. I strive to make this simple for you so you don't have a million steps to follow. So, I'll offer you three steps for doing it well and three steps for having fun in each chapter. Surely, you can do three steps, right?

The Well-Fun-Now Process

The following process will help you focus on the here and now.

Do It Well

1. When you feel anxiety, stress, pressure, panic, etc., **step back (mentally) and listen** to the voice in your head that's telling you something that creates the emotions you're feeling. Typically these voices will say things like, "I'm going to get fired," or "She will break up with me," or "If I'm hearing voices, I must be crazy."

2. **Recognize the error** in your thinking and the lack of control you have over the future. You don't know if you'll get fired. You don't know if she will break up with you. You only know that you have a challenge in front of you that needs to be addressed.

3. **Take responsibility** for those things you can do. If you can work on the project, do so. If you can apologize to your girlfriend, do so. If you have prescription drugs that will make the voices go away, you should take them. Let go of that which you cannot control.

Make It Fun

1. When you realize that you are creating the stress yourself, and it's not related to any reality, you should hit yourself in the nose for thinking such things. OK, not really, but it's fun for me to think that you might. Seriously, **find a fun mantra** to reinforce the disconnect. I like to say, "Heather Locklear." It not only breaks me out of the cycle of anxiety, it gives me a much nicer image on which to focus.

2. **Call a trusted friend** to help talk you down off the anxiety ledge. My colleague and business partner David Glickman and I always try to answer the phone with something funny when either of us calls the other (thanks to caller ID). That funny line might be all I need to break me out of my misdirected thinking.

3. Once you determine what you can do, try to **make the process as fun** as possible. If I have a project due and I'm going to be working all night, I'll turn on my favorite tunes and buy something fun to eat so that the process of the

project is as tolerable as possible. If I have an article due, I'll go to the coffee (local) shop, where I can enjoy the scenery of people coming and going while I tap into my creativity.

Dealing with the now is actually dealing with the real reality, not the reality in our heads. As much as we love the past and fear the future, it is the now that provides the rich opportunities in life. If we do the now well and make the now fun, our future will be enhanced and our past will be less important.

Chapter 3

Have Character, Don't Be One

In a standup routine, Steve Martin said that the phrase "I forgot" can come in handy in a variety of situations. For instance, he said, "If you get arrested for armed robbery, you can simply tell the judge, 'I forgot armed robbery was illegal.'"

I love that routine. But it's a bit too close to home these days. It seems that our elected officials, corporate CEOs, and Hollywood stars have forgotten that bad values are not *really* in their best interest.

Have you ever wondered where our values come from? They come from our surroundings. They come from our parents. They come from our teachers. They come from television, peers, and faith —and sometimes, unfortunately, in that order. But if parents, teachers, television, peers, and faith do not instill the proper values in us, we can't live up to our greatest potential.

Now I'm not trying to be some-holier-than-thou, my-values-are-better-than-yours, ethical giant. I've made some very bad decisions in my life. And I would love to delete those experiences from my hard drive. But in keeping with focusing on the now, I can't obsess about those mistakes. Instead, I work very hard to live a value-driven life in spite of my shortcomings in the past. By doing so, I sleep better, I have a positive effect on others, and ultimately, I serve less time in prison.

My values came from my family and the part of the country where I grew up. My formative years were spent in the small town of Emory, Virginia. To be truthful, it wasn't really a town. It was smaller—just a wide spot in the road. Basically it was a community of about 280 people, most of whom were associated with Emory and Henry College, a small Methodist college in the Appalachian Mountains.

In Emory, everybody knew everyone. And since my father was the vice president of the college, we were celebrities—that is, in a small Appalachian community kind of way. So at age 18, when I bought my first *Playboy* magazine, partly for the great in-depth articles and partly because at 18, I legally could, I cased the store several times, making sure I didn't see anyone I knew. Ultimately, my mother knew about my purchase before I even got back to my car. That's how word of mouth, or word of mothers, works in small, almost-towns.

But from the perspective of creating solid values, small towns are the best teachers. There were opportunities to live out good values all around us. My father was a lifelong Rotarian. My mother was a member of several community clubs. And all three of my siblings did volunteer work.

So I, too, am very service minded, currently spending about one quarter of my time in community service through Rotary, my church, my kids' activities, and my professional association.

Being Prepared . . . For Service

I was a Boy Scout, and I'm proud to say that my son Ryan is also involved in scouting and is about to receive his Eagle Scout Award. Today, though, scouting does not have the same reputation it had when I was young. Camping, knot tying, and learning to use a knife were cool when I was growing up. Wearing a khaki uniform and an funky neckerchief was a bit odd, but we were certainly not outcasts. Today, scouts can be ridiculed for being nerds and weirdos.

One night my wife, Wendy, and I were going out to dinner with friends. Earlier in the week, Ryan had asked us not to tell the other couple that he was at scout camp because they had a daughter in his grade and he didn't want her to know he was a Boy Scout. So we covered for him and told them he was at Navy Seal Camp. While it has become a funny joke in our family, it is disappointing that scouting doesn't have a better reputation, because it has sure taught us great values.

After high school I attended the University of Virginia and joined a national service fraternity, Alpha Phi Omega (APO). Coincidentally, but not my reason for joining, APO was founded by former Boy Scouts who wanted to continue their focus on service in college. Our chapter of APO did a service project in the community every Saturday morning for the entire school year. I think back on that now and am amazed that we could pull that off, as we were mostly irresponsible, immature, and often inebriated college students. But we learned to do service well, and we had a lot of fun along the way.

My father was in Rotary for over 50 years, and as a child I saw all the good things that Rotary did in our community. Today, I'm a Rotarian as well. Our motto is "Service Above Self," and as Rotarians, we embrace a fascinating principle called The Four-Way Test. It goes like this:

> Of everything we think, say, and do,
>
> Is it the Truth?
>
> Is it fair to all concerned?
>
> Will it build goodwill and better friendships?
>
> Is it beneficial to all concerned?

When we're committed to a principle like that, it changes the way we live. It's very other centered. In fact, in my club, whenever we make fun of someone else or mention the name of our business, we're fined a dollar. It's a simple and fun way to remind us that it's not about us. I'm proud to be a Rotarian. And I don't even have to wear a neckerchief . . . or a fez.

Principles Are Value-able

A number of years ago, I read an article in *Golf Digest* magazine about a young man named Charles Siem. At age 18, he was playing in a series of tournaments in which he was predicted to win. After sinking the final putt to win one of the preliminary tournaments, he discovered that somewhere on the course, he had played someone else's ball. If you're not familiar with the rules of golf, it's typically expected that a player hit his own ball. But no one else knew that Charles had played the wrong ball. He could have easily pocketed the ball and accepted the trophy. Instead, he walked up to the tournament officials and explained what had happened. He was disqualified and did not win the tournament.

Charles made a value-based decision. And surprisingly, at the young age of 18, he became a role model for the rest of us. Even though he knew the cost, he took responsibility by doing the right thing. We should all strive to be like Charles.

People Can See Your True You Through Your Values

A man named Bob was on his way home from work. He stopped at his friend Fred's house to pick up a casserole dish Fred's wife had borrowed. Bob sat down in the kitchen to chat for a minute while Fred washed the dish. Fred's wife, Marjorie, was also in the kitchen preparing dinner.

While Fred was drying the dish, he looked at Marjorie and said, "You are just the most beautiful woman I have ever known. And you take such good care of me and the kids. I love you very much."

A few minutes later, Bob pulled Fred aside and said, "What was that all about?"

Fred said, "I started being more complimentary a few months ago, and it has done more to improve my marriage than anything else I've ever done."

Bob suddenly realized how rarely he complimented his own wife and decided he should try to improve.

Upon arriving home, Bob went straight into the kitchen where his wife, Betty, was fixing dinner. He walked right up to her and said, "You look gorgeous. That dinner smells great. And the kitchen is so clean."

Betty immediately started crying.

Bob said, "What's wrong?"

Betty said, "You just don't realize what a bad day I've had. We woke up late this morning. Then, on my way to drop off the kids at school, I had a flat tire. Both kids missed their first class. On the way home, the school nurse called to let me know that while running to her second class, Mary fell down the stairs and hurt her arm. The nurse said I should take Mary to the ER to get it checked out. We sat in the ER for three and half hours before being seen. Then we sat in the exam room for another four hours. Thank goodness her arm was only sprained. But I just got home a few minutes ago. I'm trying to throw something edible together for dinner. And then to top the day off, you come home drunk."

Walk the talk. We can't let our good values be a surprise to others!

What Do Values Look Like?

Stephen Covey wrote in his book, *The 7 Habits of Highly Effective People*, that we should make a list of our values and put them in front of us where we'll see them every day. Below are the values that I strive to embrace. The first list includes values I embrace for my personal life, and the second list represents the principles for my business.

My Values

My Personal Values:

- Appreciation
- Balance
- Compassion
- Excellence
- Fairness
- Fun
- Honesty
- Humility
- Professionalism
- Respect
- Responsibility
- Self-improvement

My Work Principles:

- I serve others.
- My work is based on commonsense principles presented in a funny way.
- I volunteer as part of my work, not in addition to it.
- I make a good living.
- My business model is not complicated.
- The results of my work lead to more work.

As you can see, these values and principles are designed to make me both a better person and a better businessman. But I can't benefit from these ideals unless I follow them. For instance, I can't embrace the value of compassion if I'm rude to people. I can't embrace the value of self-improvement if I'm not objective about where I need to improve. And I can't embrace the value of honesty if I lie about my income on my tax returns.

Once we start being dishonest, it's hard to get back on track. It's that tangled-web issue. So, we're better off not going down that path at all. For instance, one of the most difficult honesty questions a man gets asked is when his wife or girlfriend asks, "Does this dress make me look fat?"

I've determined that in this particular situation, we MUST be honest. So, I will simply say, "No. That dress doesn't make you look fat. That sleeve of Girl Scout cookies you ate last night makes you look fat. The dress has nothing to do with it."

See what I mean? We *can* be true to our values in even the most difficult circumstances.

The Well-Fun-Values Process

So, how do values help us do it well and make it fun on a day-to-day basis? Basically, they guide our decision making. Whether at work or home, values help us make the right decisions rather than the easy decisions. It's that simple. And whether we're willing to admit it or not, our values define who we are. The great UCLA basketball coach John Wooden said, "Your character is who you really are, while you're reputation is simply what others think you are."

I read that Quakers have certain principles by which they live and that societal norms are not enough to make them veer from these principles. For example, a Quaker testifying in court will not swear to tell the truth because doing so implies that he does not tell the truth in other situations. Since honesty is one of their strongly held beliefs, implying that they don't tell the truth would be an insult to their principles. Perhaps their strategy is a bit more solid than my telling my wife that eating Girl Scout cookies is fattening.

Here are some tips to help you embrace the value of, well, values:

Do It Well

1. **Develop a list** of values you wish to embrace. You can ask yourself how you want to be remembered as a person, a parent, a spouse, an employee, etc. This is called the Eulogy Technique because it forces us to look at our lives in retrospect as a way to carve them out in the future.

2. It's important to **put the list of values where you can see it** every day. The visual reminder is a good gut check to make sure you don't forget, as Steve Martin suggested, that armed robbery is a crime—and not on our value list.

3. When a situation arises in which you must make a decision, **consulting your values** helps you make the right decision rather than the easy decision. Staying true to our values serves not only us but others as well. And remember, it's perfectly all right to consult friends and advisors when you encounter particularly sticky situations. Better to be thorough than rush a decision and regret it. And for what it's worth, if you hear, "What the hell were you thinking?" you might have made a bad decision.

Make It Fun

1. When you're creating your list of values, you can't forget to **include the fun values** like laughter, humor, play, vacation, triple-layer chocolate cake . . . Values are not only serious but also the fun things we want to be known for. If you enjoy telling jokes, then one of your values might include

sharing humor with others as way to be more purposeful about your fun.

2. In the midst of making decisions, you should **add a fun element** to take the sting of seriousness out of the process. By asking yourself, "What would William Shatner do?" or "What would Paris Hilton *not* do?" you can turn the tables a bit.

3. **Celebrate the success** of a decision well made. Or, if your decision was wildly unpopular, you should stay inside your home until the unrest settles down. But remember, if your values are solid, it *was* the right decision.

Whether we want to admit it or not, our values are like a name tag on our lapel screaming, "This is who I am." Most of us don't realize how visible they are. But there is a value in being transparent with our values. We *should* be open and honest with others as we employ our values. Nothing is more frustrating than for someone to have a lack of understanding of our decision-making process. Once we explain how we used our principles to arrive at our decision, even those who disagree with us will have respect for our integrity.

Values. They're the principles by which we should live. Done well, our life and work have more integrity. And on some level, that's more fun.

Chapter 4

Believe It or Not

My friend and colleague John Daly was known for adding humor to his presentations on history, U.S. government, and communication. He was also a devout Catholic with eight children.

"All boys except for the four girls," he would say.

On a number of occasions, John shared the following prayer that he heard at a national postal convention many years ago:

Dear God, may everything we do be First Class.

Please print your Zip Code upon our hearts so that we may never go astray.

Provide Special Handling for those of us who are Fragile and keep us all in one piece.

We have been Signed, Sealed, Stamped, and Delivered in your image and we beg that you keep us in your care as we go about our Appointed Rounds.

And when our days draw to a close and we are marked

"Return to Sender," be there to greet us at Heaven's door so that nobody may ever say , "Undeliverable at This Address."

Amen

This poignant and humorous sentiment will always be one of my fond memories of John, who died in 2009. And it is an excellent example of the intermingling of faith and fun.

In the Beginning

I was raised Methodist and attended the Emory United Methodist Church. I am now Presbyterian. There was never a time when I was not a believer in God, Jesus, and Billy Graham. The church youth group was an important training ground for my faith. It was my primary social network when I was in both elementary school and high school, and my friends shared many of the same values, mostly derived from our Methodist beliefs. We had fun weekly meetings, studied the Bible, and participated in service projects in our community. I visited sick people, took food to the underprivileged, and even painted a mural on the wall of a state psychiatric hospital, all because of my association with the church youth group.

Two experiences from my youth group stood out. First, we made a movie about the Ten Commandments. In the style of Cecil B. DeMille, we cut and pasted thousands of frames of Super 8 footage depicting both the good way to follow the commandments and the not-so-good way. From being pushed out a window for the murder commandment to pretending to be naked for the adultery commandment (our youth leaders suggested we not depict this commandment any more realistically than that), we displayed our Thou Shalts in a big way. It was a very fun and funny way to not only learn the Ten Commandments but also to learn how to work together to produce a surprisingly good-quality movie. The faith lesson here is that it can be fun to learn more about our faith. It doesn't have to be stern Sunday school teachers reading passages from the Bible in an outdated language that makes no sense. I probably learned more about a model lifestyle by making our *Ten Commandments* than I ever have by trying to read about the Ten Commandments by myself.

The second most memorable youth experience I had was participating in a mission trip with Mountain T.O.P. (Tennessee Outreach Project). For a week in the summer, we worked on the yards and houses of underprivileged people in the mountains of Tennessee. For the first time in my life, I witnessed what real poverty was like. And yet these people were not angry about their situations or jealous of those who had more. They appreciated everything they had and were grateful for all we did for them. They also had a faith that sustained them even when their material needs were barely met.

It was an extraordinary experience and I remember coming home with a different view of the world—as if God had awakened something inside of me by giving me the eyes to see my world through His eyes.

This is what faith is to me. It's a belief in something bigger than us. It's a confidence in a bigger plan and a synchronization of the world beyond our comprehension. It is not logical or tangible but is the essence of hope, love, and joy.

Now, I will be the first to admit that believing in God is very hard for me. I'm someone who likes proof. I like evidence. I like to touch it and feel it. I've never had a burning-bush experience and I can't even turn water into decent lemonade. But somehow, there is something inside of me that believes that what we see in the world on a daily basis is not all there is.

Eckhart Tolle says that we all have an innate desire to connect with our creator. Different religions call it different things, but I agree that it's there and it drives us to seek a place of greater spiritual enlightenment. When we do, we get out of our self-centeredness and look toward God and others with a loving and compassionate attitude.

So how does this help us to do things well? Or have more fun? I'm glad you asked.

Making Faith Real

My faith teaches me certain principles that help me live right. And by "right," I mean with integrity. Of course the Ten Commandments are the big ones. Most of these are pretty easy to follow even though the adultery commandment seems to trip a lot of folks up.

Long after the Ten Commandments were handed down, Jesus came along and taught us a few new principles. Basically, Jesus said that love and compassion were the trump cards when it comes to our faith. He said we should love God and love our neighbors. And by neighbors, he didn't just mean the young attractive single neighbor who's easy to love. He also meant the grumpy, anal-retentive guy who measures the height of our grass when we don't mow it. Neighbor, to Jesus, meant everybody. And then he told us to tell everyone about Him. That's the part that irritates a lot of our non-Christian brothers and sisters—especially when we suggest that they might go to Hell if they don't believe exactly as we do. I'm not so sure Jesus would have put it exactly that way.

I lean toward the St. Francis of Assisi perspective, as when he said, "Preach the Gospel. And if necessary, use words."

He's saying that we should let our actions be the demonstration of our faith. And that's how faith works for me. It encourages me to *behave* a certain way—hopefully with compassion and concern for others—not to tell *others* how to behave.

I attended several Promise Keepers events back in the 1990s. These were stadium events founded by former University of Colorado coach Bill McCartney. There was controversy about these events because some people thought they were designed to put men in a position of power over women and children. That couldn't have been farther from the truth. Instead, these events held up a mirror to men and showed them how they had not been good husbands, fathers, and friends. After beating us down with the truth, the speakers, music, and prayer lifted us back up with the motivation to go back home and become better men.

That's what faith should do. It should lead us toward betterment. It should not put us in a place of the oppressor or the narcissistic tyrant. Faith is about a humble confidence.

Another outcome of my faith journey is the development of personal accountability partnerships. I have an addictive personality and I can easily become addicted to just about anything—alcohol, food, sex, television, Cinnabons, Angry Birds, etc. And if you know anything about addictive tendencies, you know that it's very hard to fight them off on our own. That's why the Alcoholics Anonymous model is so effective. It places alcoholics with sponsors who have been in their shoes. The partnering helps the addict feel less alone in the fight against the addiction.

Through my faith journey, I have developed several accountability partnerships. Essentially, these relationships were based on open, frank discussions between the two of us about our lives, our marriages, our parenting, our Cinnabons, and anything else that needed improvement, by shining a light on our lives in the presence of someone else. It's like confession and repentance all wrapped up in one great meeting at Starbucks. If we feel isolated, uncertain, or frustrated with our faith, we look for someone who can support us and make our journey less lonely.

Faith is about inspiration, integrity, and accountability—all designed to make us better at living our lives. Even when we get to the end of our lives, our faith can make the process bearable, more meaningful, and amazingly, more fun.

In the End, Amen to Faith

My friend Roz Trieber was battling terminal cancer. As a humorist, she always saw the up side of life even when she was dying. When she entered into the hospice program, she scheduled a visit with the hospice's rabbi even though she was already a member of a local congregation. Then, she decided to see what the Christian chaplain had to offer. She told me, "I wanted to see all of my options."

Roz was secure in her faith but realized she could learn from other spiritual mentors during this challenging time in her life. I believe it was her faith that taught her that principle.

At her funeral, I learned that Roz had invited many friends to her house at her family's annual Seder dinner. During this Passover meal, she often taught her non-Jewish friends what each part of the meal meant and, eventually, they were participating in the service as well. Roz used her faith to connect with others. Roz did it well. And along the way, she was and had great fun.

Holy Humor?

I hope you can see that our faith can be a wonderful grounding when it comes to keeping our eyes on what's important. But it can also be a great connection to a source of joy. Being faithful certainly doesn't mean being uptight and overly serious, even when we're serious about our faith. I believe that humor is a gift from God and should be used generously. In fact many of the parables in the Bible were intended to be funny, as they were absurd at the time of their telling.

For instance, when Jesus said that a rich man getting into heaven was more difficult than a camel going through the eye of a needle, this would have been a funny metaphor. Today, we don't get it because the context is different. But Jesus was using absurdity to teach a point. That's holy humor at its best.

In our family, we rotate the nightly dinner blessing among each family member (my wife, my kids, and me). Once when my daughter Caitlin was about six, she said, "Now I lay me down to eat. Ooops."

We lost it.

It wasn't sacrilegious, nor was it a disrespect to our faith. It was just funny.

The Well-Fun-Faith Process

The challenge of faith is that it involves so much, well, faith. We can't physically touch God but we can see the results of God—that is, if we believe in God. Someone once compared it to the wind. We can't see the wind but we can see its impact. Therefore we know it's there.

Whether we have a strong faith, a weak faith, or no faith in a higher being, it's important that something bigger than we are leads us through our life. Otherwise, it will just be us deciding about what is right or wrong, and no offense, but who says we're the best judge of that?

Here are a few suggestions that will make your faith journey a bit less burdensome:

Do It Well

1. **Never be satisfied** with your current level of faith. We all should seek more enlightenment, knowledge, and awareness when it comes to our faith or our belief system. This doesn't mean trying to deconstruct our beliefs but to make them real and more meaningful to us. We can do this through books, spiritual mentors, and places of worship.

2. **Find time each day to meditate, pray, or chew your faith cud** (that's an Appalachian form of meditation). Our quiet time helps us to get out of the hectic pace of our daily routine so we can focus on the important rather than the urgent and unimportant.

3. **Find a spiritual mentor**, an accountability partner, or a small group of folks who share your beliefs. These people will not only become a great source of support for your life, but they will also help you to maintain your faith and life goals by helping to keep you focused on the right things.

Make It Fun

1. **Lighten up about your faith.** We live in a diverse world with a lot of different faith perspectives. If we're so caught up in the rightness of our faith, we won't be able to see beyond the nose on our face. Remember, we can't get the speck out of someone else's eye if we don't see the big hunking piece of dirt in our own eye.

2. **Look for the humor within your own faith.** Jon Acuff wrote a wonderful book called *Stuff Christians Like,* full of introspective humor about the wacky things that Christians do. While a bit irreverent, he has to be secure in his faith to be able to laugh at it.

3. **Pray for your sense of humor.** God clearly had a sense of humor, or else he wouldn't have given us one, nor would He have put so many funny things in the world. If we look for the humor around us, it reinforces the humor that God gave us.

I have faith in you to have faith in your faith. If we do it well while having some fun, our life will be richer—in a humble, other-centered kind of way.

Chapter 5

You're Pretty Good at That

E arly in my life, I learned about the value of practice.

I made the JV basketball team in 9th grade. But at 5' 3" tall with no specific dribbling or shooting skills, I was not a candidate for a college scholarship. In fact, during my illustrious high school career, I averaged 20 seconds of playing time per game and .2 points per game. That means I had to play five games to score a point. Not that I actually scored partial points, I'm just pointing out the lackluster quality of my game.

One day during basketball practice, I jumped a high hurdle that was sitting next to the court. The track coach saw me do this and said, "Culberson [since coaches are required by their national coaches' association to only use last names], you could run track. You're fast and you have really good form on the hurdles."

Apparently, his eyesight was bad. How could a 5' 3" kid be good at high hurdles? High hurdles are 39" high. I was 63" tall. That means the top of the hurdle was only 24" from the top of my head. Clearly, if I was to run track, I would be *jumping* the high hurdles.

Ironically, I ended up running high *and* intermediate hurdles as well as competing in the high jump. I know. Lots of high for someone with lots of short. By the way, in case you're curious, they start the high jump competition at 5' 1". I refer you back to the previous paragraph where I listed my height at 5'3". I was pretty much out of the high jump competition by the second round.

Luckily, I discovered that I was good at tennis and height wasn't a barrier to playing tennis. I made the JV team in ninth grade, and by tenth grade, I was the number-one tennis player in my high school, primarily because the five guys who were better than me graduated the same year. I played all the time. The problem was, I didn't practice enough with the right kind of people, and I didn't practice the right things. Since I was the best player in my high school, no one could challenge me. So I practiced but didn't get better. Thus, when we played other schools, I was over my head in that position, and I rarely won (2 wins and 9 losses, in case you have me in your fantasy league).

Marching band was a different story. I was the top baritone horn player in the band. Not baritone sax, but baritone horn. It wasn't a sexy instrument. I never saw a girl in high school flutter her eyes and say, "Oh, he's dreamy. He plays baritone horn."

But I was good.

In my senior year, I made first alternate in the all-state band tryouts. The reason I didn't *make* the all-state band was again related to practice. I was already good, so I didn't overdo it in the practicing department. However, because I didn't study tempos closely enough, I misread the sight-reading portion of the auditions and played a song roughly 26 times slower than it should have been played. I got nice comments from the judges on my tone and breathing but my pacing failed in a big way.

So, what's my point? Well, if you've read Malcolm Gladwell's book *Outliers* (and if you haven't, you should), you'll recall that he discusses a study indicating that it takes about 10,000 hours of practice to become really good at something. I'm talking Tiger Woods good or Rafael Nadal good. Clearly, to be proficient with our skills, whether God-given or learned, we need to practice, practice, practice. That applies to getting to Carnegie Hall as well (sorry, old bad joke).

Developing the Skill of Skill Development

Most of us think we're better than we are. When I ask members of my audiences to raise their hands if they consider themselves a bad driver, usually about 1% of them raise their hands. However when I ask if they *know* a bad driver, 95% of them raise their hands. See how this works? We think *we're* good and everybody *else* needs improvement. And since we're already relatively good, we don't think we need to practice or develop our skills further. It's those other people who need to brush up on their sorely lacking skills.

So, if I may be so bold, I'm going to suggest that we are not as good at our jobs *or* our lives as we think we are. And if, at the end of our life, we want to look back with as few regrets as possible, we need to work on those areas.

Consider an example of being the best. Once on the Academy Awards, Steve Martin and Tina Fey presented the screenwriter's award. Most presenters would not put much work into a one-minute introduction, but as screenwriters, comedians, and talented professionals, Martin and Fey did. Here is the opening to their dialogue:

"I'm Steve Martin."

"And I'm Tina Fey."

"And I'm Steve Martin."

Brilliant.

It was a simple interaction with a supposed oneupmanship that led to a hilarious reaction. And I'm sure they spent a lot of time writing *and* rehearsing it. But to us, it looks simple and easy—*because* they put the necessary time into it up front.

Later in the presentation, Tina Fey said, "It has been said that to write is to live forever."

To which Steve Martin responded, "The man who wrote that is dead."

Later, Steve was introducing another award. Tina Fey was looking at him as he spoke. He stopped, did a double take, and said, "Do *NOT* fall in love with me."

Three brilliant lines, perfectly delivered. It's obvious that Steve Martin and Tina Fey put in their 10,000 hours of practice to get to the top of their game. And most of us would write it off as innate talent. That's why we remain content with our own mediocre, or at best, good performance. We assume we don't have the innate talent or can't develop it.

Jim Collins said that good is the enemy of great because if we're good, we don't think we need to improve. Similarly, one of my graduate school professors, Martin Schwartz said, "Just when you think you know it all is when you need to go back to school."

I'm good at humor. But I could be better.

I'm a bad snowboarder. And I could definitely be better.

I'm OK as a parent, spouse, business owner, and on, and on, and on.

Get it? We could be better. And my belief is that when we're better, we're more fulfilled *and* we enrich the lives of those around us.

If we're a better manager, we make it better for our staff.

If we're a better parent, our kids benefit.

If we're a better get-betterer, we'll get better at getting better. And that's better for everyone.

Now, I'm not suggesting that we need to be good at everything. Nobody can do that. However, I am suggesting that we can be better at the specific roles in our life and the responsibilities we have.

Squirrelly Skills

A few weeks ago, I removed a privacy fence from our deck. Once the privacy fence was gone, I had a great view of my backyard. So, I moved my desk in front of the window to get a better perspective on this great new view—and clearly to distract me from all the things I should be doing instead of gazing mindlessly at my backyard.

It didn't take long to realize that a perfect addition to my new view would be a couple of bird feeders strategically placed in my yard. I installed new feeders complete with anti-squirrel mechanisms and and sat back in my office waiting for the birds. For three days, I didn't see any birds. I checked the feeders to make sure the birds could get to the food and discovered a huge pile of seed on the ground below the feeders

This meant one thing.

Squirrels.

I replaced the food, and the next morning, I got no work done while I stared at the feeders for nearly an hour. Sure enough, a squirrel climbed the pole and practically emptied the feeder onto the ground. I ran outside and chased him away. I brought the feeders inside and attached a more elaborate squirrel protection system. But if you've ever dealt with squirrels, you know that nothing is truly squirrel resistant. Squirrels are too smart. They've put in their 10,000 hours of outsmarting squirrel-resistant devices.

It took an hour to install the new dome protection device at just the right height to provide a barrier to the squirrels. It took the squirrels 27 seconds to figure out how to use the other feeder pole to jump onto the new device, grab the pole, swing sideways, and then eat all of the birdseed.

So I moved the feeder poles farther apart and raised the device higher. This went on for three days.

By the third day of adjustments, the squirrels couldn't jump high enough to get to the feeder or on top of the dome. I sat in my office with a prideful grin on my face, still not doing any work, as I watched the stupid smaller-brain-than-mine squirrels fail time and time again.

Then, in Cirque du Soleil style, a squirrel came flying through the air from a branch on a nearby tree and landed on top of my feeder pole. He (and I say *he,* hoping that female squirrels don't act this fool-ishly) grabbed the top of the pole, hung upside down, and drained the feeder for himself and all the other squirrels.

I'm embarrassed to say that I lowered my head, stood up, and gave him a standing ovation. I had been defeated.

Or had I?

I put domes on top of the feeders, on the side and underneath, barely making them accessible to even the smallest of birds. I sat in my office and waited while I simultaneously searched the Internet for anti-squirrel submachine guns.

Eventually, the squirrels gave up and returned to dropping acorns on the roof of my house. I may be a mediocre hurdler, but apparently I've become a highly skilled squirrel fighter.

Squirrels are skilled. And they don't usually give up until they improve upon their skills enough to get them what they want. We humans, on the other hand, tend to give up too quickly, often set-tling for less than we want. I hate to say it, but we should learn from the squirrels. If you had a squirrel's determination, what would you work on?

The Well-Fun-Skills Process

Figuring out how to improve our skills is not that tough, but some-times, we're too close to it and can't be objective. So, let's pretend we're a squirrel to make it easier. This will be easier for some of us than others.

Do It Well

1. Determine what your nut (or your birdseed) is. In other words, **what is an immediate goal for your life or work?** What do you need to accomplish or what do you strive to be? Perhaps it's becoming a manager. Or maybe you'd like

to learn how to ski. You might even want to make ceramic squirrels for your yard because you just can't get enough of those cute furry creatures. Then write down your goals. Don't forget the easily forgettable goals, like being a better spouse and parent.

2. In order to get your nut, **what skills do you need**? Rather than running, scurrying up trees, and outsmarting humans, what are the obvious technical abilities you need for your particular goals and the not-so-obvious abilities, such as communication, organization, typing, running meetings, etc.?

3. **Determine how to get these skills**. Will you get an advanced degree? Will you read the most recent best seller on the topic? Will you hire a mentor? Will you attend a conference or a seminar? Create priorities and deadlines for the plan and then follow through.

Make It Fun

1. Improving skills can be tough and at times discouraging. In order to make the process more enjoyable, **consider pursuing these improvements with a colleague, friend, or family member**. Just like exercise, if you have someone with you, it feels much less isolating and will keep your motivation up.

2. Remember that **all work and no play is, well, work**. We all need to balance our skill-improvement process with fun and play. Just as there are sports, band programs, and drama clubs to balance the curriculum in schools, it's always possible to do fun things while improving.

3. **Reward yourself for successes**. When you reach a goal or a benchmark in your improvement process, consider a reward

to pat yourself on the back for the improvement. Go simple with an ice cream cone or a gourmet cupcake, or go big with a trip to Italy. You be the judge, based on what floats your boat. You just need to make sure the rewards are the carrots to keep you improving.

Doing things well is about excellence. Excellence is about practicing the things we're good at and about improving the things we're not good at. If we embrace this concept, we will enrich our lives and the lives of those around us.

Chapter 6

It's All in Your Head . . . Sort Of

When I was 13 years old, my family went tubing. If you haven't had the pleasure, tubing involves stuffing your hindquarters into the middle of the inner tube of a tractor tire while you glide peacefully down a river enjoying the calm current and beautiful scenery. At least that's how it's supposed to be. For me, it's a personal hell that haunts me to this day.

There are two reasons I don't like tubing. First, I'm terrified of snakes, snapping turtles, and anything else that might lurk in the murky waters under my tube. Second, I've seen the movie *Deliverance*. I don't need a Ned-Beattyesque experience in the backwoods of southwest Virginia. In fact, on that fateful summer day in 1974, I had offered to stay home to keep an eye on our valuables. But my parents reminded me that we had no valuables, so I was forced to go along for the ride. Thus began a psychological trauma of "Dueling Banjos" proportions.

Shortly after we "put in," we encountered our first run of rapids. I quickly discovered that my body was not well suited for tubing. Not only did I continually slip through the tube, because of the simple fact that my slight yet chiseled ninety-pound physique didn't fill the hole, but also I had no natural padding to protect me from the four thousand or so river rocks scattered throughout the rapids. I bottomed out a dozen times, causing bruises all over my backside—which could have been just the evidence I needed for Social Services to place me in a non-tubing family. I complained about the rocks, but my brother just told me to "grow up" and "act like a man." It occurs to me that I don't even act like a man today, so I'm sure it was an unrealistic expectation at 13.

After barely surviving rapids, we hit a deep, slow section of the river. During the slow sections, I had a lot of time to think, and when in deep, slow water, I tended to think about what else might be in the very same deep, slow water. It was the scaredest I had ever been . . . that is, until we floated around the next bend.

I could hear the others yelling about something in the river and warning us to steer clear. All I could see was what appeared to be a large balloon. In fact, it resembled that Porky Pig balloon in the Macy's Thanksgiving Day Parade. As I got closer, however, I realized it was no balloon.

It was a pig. A *real* pig. A real *dead* pig.

And apparently, it had been there for a quite some time, because it had *swolled* up, as we would say, filled with dead pig gas, to the size of a small southwest Virginia mobile home. And what was worse, the river current was taking me right toward it.

Panic set in. My first reaction was involuntary. But we were in water, so it was OK. Next, I began to thrash my legs and arms about as if my life and future psychological well-being depended on one simple outcome—getting my bruised bottom out of that river and onto the safety of the shore. I knew if I hit that pig, I would be the guy at future family reunions where people would stand off to the side and say, "You know, he weren't right ever since he hit that pig."

Luckily, I had attended summer swim camp a few years earlier and was quite an effective thrasher. After an exhausting two minutes of Olympic-caliber helicopter strokes, I skirted the pig, reached shallower water, and dove for the bank.

I stood there shaking as I watched the one tuber behind me turn the bend. It was my mother. And bless her heart, she was not so lucky.

You see, my mother never learned to swim—or to thrash, for that matter. And while her natural buoyancy would keep her afloat if she fell out of her tube, she had no ability to coordinate her limbs in any one direction. The more she flailed, the less effective she was. It was like watching a car sliding on ice. Nothing anyone could do. Except scream, that is. So my mother screamed her way right into the underbelly of that swollen swine.

As she made contact, a loud burst of gas exploded from some hidden opening on the pig. Then, the tightened skin sprang back and propelled her back across the water and slammed her onto the shore right behind me. Frantically, she picked up her tube and declared that she'd meet us at the car four miles down the road. Of course, I went with her, thus avoiding the chance of running into another one of Old MacDonald's missing friends farther downstream.

Since that sunny afternoon in my thirteenth year, I have never tubed in a river again. Neither has my mother. In fact, she'll break out in hives at just the smell of bacon cooking. And while it wasn't quite as intense as *Deliverance*, I sure do have a greater respect for Ned Beatty.

I share my tubing trauma with you because it's the perfect, albeit graphic, example of life and stress. Life is like a river. There are rapids, rocks, slow sections, deep sections, and an occasional dead pig. We never know what's around the bend, but if we're successful in journeying along the river of life, we will not fight the natural flow but instead, discover how to maneuver *with* it. And if we don't? We'll hit the pig. Worse yet, we'll *be* the pig.

So, one of the most critical ways of doing life well and making it fun is to manage ourselves when it comes to stress. No matter who we are or what we do, stress is lurking in the murky water, waiting to take us over. We need to prepare ourselves for inevitability.

The Mathematics of Stress

Years ago, I began using a formula to explain the effects of stress. Math was one of my best subjects in college, and my undergraduate advisor suggested I take more math to raise my overall grade point average. But I couldn't justify it. It's not like they're constantly inventing new numbers. Once I got through calculus, what else did I really need in everyday life? I'm not a calculator-on-the-belt type of person. It reminds me of a T-shirt I saw in *Mental Floss* magazine. It read, "I'm an English major. You do the math."

That being said, there is an equation that explains stress and it's quite simple. It looks like this:

$$\text{Stressor} + \text{Interpretation} = \text{Effects of Stress}$$

Surprisingly, stress is not inherently stressful. Instead, stress is created by our *interpretation* of the "stressor"—an event or an experience in our lives. If stress were inherently stressful, then the same things would cause stress for everyone. I'm a bit OCD (or CDO in alphabetical order, as it should be, according to another OCD friend). And since most people are not annoyed by wrinkled socks, like I am, I must assume that it is our interpretation of the stressor that makes it stressful to us.

So, if I interpret something as stressful, it will create a stress-full effect in me, and then I'll have to figure out how to cope with it. If I don't interpret it as stressful, then there is no stress effect and no need to cope.

So, how do we manage this stress formula to create less stress in our lives? Simple. We choose *how* we see every situation.

That's it. Just choose rather than react to our kneeflexes (automatic knee-jerk reflexes that are ingrained so that we respond without thinking). I know. Easier said than done. That's why I'm writing this book instead of demonstrating it to you in person. Because I have kneeflexes too. But the formula does work. And if we change our perspective *and* see the humor, it works even better.

Losing More than My Mind

One day after I turned thirty, I was in the bathroom studying the dense growth of hair on the back of my neck. Then my eyes drifted upwards and I saw, for the first time, a bald spot on my head the size of a Denny's silver dollar pancake. Based on the concentric rings, I determined it had been there for about a year.

Old family photographs confirmed my worst fear. Both of my grandfathers, who died before I was born, were totally bald, and one of my grandmothers looked like her hair was getting little thin. Since the gene skips a generation, I knew it was only a matter of time before my bald spot merged with my forehead to create a skin peninsula that would eventually work its way down to my ears.

I cut a lock of hair and placed it in the safe deposit box, figuring if Walt Disney could be unfrozen, maybe my hair could be telegenetically reborn at some later date. Then I decided to face the problem head on, so to speak, and proclaimed to my wife, Wendy, that balding was natural and I was going to accept the head that God gave me.

"Would you at least consider using Rogaine®?" she responded.

Wait a minute.

That's not the right answer.

I was looking for "I'll love you no matter how you look" or even "I think bald-headed men are sexy." I was not expecting, "For God's sake, do what you can to stop the balding!"

I considered my options. I could try Rogaine. It was easy to use and had very few side effects. However, the label did warn that if my head turned red and peeled, I should stop using it. Duh.

Propecia® was also an option. This was a drug that, when given to men with swollen prostates, grew hair. That's odd. A medicine for an organ on the opposite end of my body grows hair on my head.

The thought of being called Prostate Head reminded me too much of high school

I thought about using Miracle-Gro. It had done wonders for our azaleas, while also keeping the aphids away, but it was not yet FDA approved for hair growth as far as I knew. Too bad.

Then there was a hair transplant. This was a procedure where "plugs" of hair from one part of your head are relocated to drilled holes in the balding area. That reminded me of a friend who bought a Christmas tree that was bare on one side. He drilled holes in the trunk and then transplanted severed limbs from the fuller side of the tree. I remember looking at the tree and thinking that something was just not quite right.

Finally, I could have gotten a hairpiece. Then I could have joined the host of proud men who walked around each day thinking that no one knew they were wearing a toupee while everyone thought, "Boy, is that a bad toupee." I envisioned a full head of hair blowing in the wind . . . and me running after it.

Ultimately, I chose a double cocktail of Rogaine and Propecia. For several years, I used it religiously, and while it did not grow any new hair, it did stop the hair-loss process. Every once in a while, I thought my hair looked fuller, but Wendy quickly suggested that it was "just the light."

Dang it.

For some reason, I saw the hair loss as a personal loss. While I didn't mind the way other bald men looked, it seemed worse when it happened to me.

But by seeing situations differently or interpreting them differently, we can choose to give them much less power over us. Then, if we can actually see the humor in the situation, we add an element of fun while preventing the stress from hurting us.

Below is a letter that my 87-year-old father sent a couple of years before he died, in response to an increase in the price of eggs, to a neighborhood teenager who delivered his eggs. The increase was about 40 cents but represented a big jump in prices, at least to my father. I think this illustrates the power of combining humor with a new perspective.

Dear Mr. Stanley,

Your letter of July 11 has been received.

Due to my modest fixed income and your exorbitant, 33 1/3% increase in the price of your eggs, this letter will request you to reduce my order 33 1/3% to eight eggs each delivery. I hope the chicks will soon be productive and the price of eggs will return to normal.

Please do not make delivery of eggs to me from September 19 to September 21 since I will be on our 63rd honeymoon with MY chick.

Sincerely,
GC Culberson

And I wonder where my sense of humor comes from.

The Well-Fun-Stress Process

So, let's get down to specifics. What does this formula-fighting, humor-responding, stress management process look like? The next time we encounter a stressor, we can implement the following steps. I'll use the common experience of road rage to illustrate the process. Let's say you're running late for a meeting or an appointment and you encounter a traffic jam on your way to the meeting.

Do It Well

1. First, **identify the real stressor**. You'll have a tendency to see the traffic jam as the stressor, but in reality, you were late

to begin with. So, just as a tendency for OCD can represent an underlying stress, your frustration at the traffic represents your frustration with yourself for being late. So you need to recognize that the traffic jam is not the problem.

2. **Examine your perspective about being late**. Is it really that bad? Realize that there are worse things in the world, such as illness, war, poverty, and arriving at a Starbucks ten minutes after it closes. Putting the stress in the proper perspective helps us relieve the stress.

3. Once you realize you are stuck in the stressful situation, you can **change the faulty perspective that leads to the stress**. For instance:

    (a) The slow person in front of me is not an idiot.

    (b) I probably won't get fired for being late.

    (c) Ramming the car in front of me won't make me feel better.

    (d) There are many worse things than being late. Thinking of them makes me grateful.

Make It Fun

1. **Occupying your mind with funny thoughts** can help you to break out of stress-full thinking. For instance, when one of my flights was late because of a burned-out bulb in the cockpit, I tried to come up with the answer to the following: How many pilots does it take to change a lightbulb? It forced my mind into a funny place.

2. **Look for the humor that's around you.** The following are funny things I've seen in stressful situations:

   (a) A piece of spinach in the teeth of someone who was yelling at me.

   (b) A bumper sticker on the slow car in front of me that read, "My C student beat up your honor student."

   (c) Someone putting on makeup while she was driving and then hitting the bumper of the person in front of her.

3. **Call a humor buddy.** I have a couple of friends who will make me laugh whenever I'm in a stressful situation. They help me get out of myself and put things in the proper perspective.

If we follow the formula and realize that our perspective is the biggest contributor to our stress, we can change our perspective and then, get this, *change our stress*. It's a no-brainer.

Chapter 7

You Are What You Reap

At age 10, I was hit by a car. It was *not* my fault. I was walking home after playing pool with some friends when a man drove too close to the shoulder and hit me. I'm not sure if he didn't see me or if he was more focused on the car approaching in the opposite lane. He *was* elderly and I *was* thin.

I was in the hospital for five weeks in a medieval corrective contraption called traction. Then, I was in a full leg cast for another six weeks. By the time I got out of the cast, my withered leg was weak and immobile. I needed physical therapy to regain my strength and mobility. So my parents made an appointment with the best (and the only) physical therapist in town, Dr. Ed Hill.

Dr. Hill was old school. He sported a tidy crew cut, he wore tight T-shirts with rolled-up sleeves that revealed several tattoos, and he had a stub of a cigar in his mouth at all times. To a 10-year-old kid, he was intimidating. For an adult, he was intimidating.

Upon arriving for my first visit, he asked me to get on the exam table (and by "exam table," I mean "place of torture and dismemberment"), lie on my back, and bend my bad leg as far as I could. I bent it about 10 degrees and that was it.

He growled at me to "bend it more."

Spittle flew from his mouth, but his cigar never moved.

I said, "I can't bend it any more than that."

I watched Dr. Hill's face turn red and the vein on his forehead pulse. Then, in a moment that still feels surreal to me, Dr. Hill raised his hand as if summoning a waiter and then he hit me square in the stomach.

My gum flew out of my mouth. And then, my reflexes kicked in. I doubled at the waist and both of my knees flew up to my chest.

"Goooood!" Dr. Hill said with a sadistic grin on his face.

My physical therapist had just tricked me into bending my leg. There was no yoga-like stretching to ease the pain of the new movement. No building up of the muscles. No M&Ms in his pocket for every inch I moved my leg. Just one shot to the gut and a 90-degree bend.

My leg was throbbing. I couldn't help wondering what was next. Nose hair removal? Water boarding? Would he make me go tubing as some sort of aquatic rehab therapy? I was terrified.

Dr. Hill's techniques never got any worse. But for the next three weeks, I did everything possible to bend my leg at home in hopes that I would escape any future pain.

No matter what Dr. Hill was thinking, there are no shortcuts to rehab or to good health, for that matter. Our well-being requires that we put in the time and energy to be healthy. But it can be fun too.

The older we get, the more our bodies pay us back for the neglect when we were younger. Weight takes its toll on our knees. The wrong diet wreaks havoc on our hearts. And Cinnabons will trick us into believing that the shirt manufacturers are using less material than they used to (a claim my brother once made to the delight of the rest of the family). My hospice experience is filled with examples of people who ignored their bodies' warnings until it was too late. I, for one, don't want to get to the end of my life and find that all I have to look forward to is sitting slumped in a chair-eating pureed prunes.

It wasn't until I turned 40 that I made some very important discoveries about my health. And while that was later than it should have been, I feel lucky to have figured a few things out.

Eat, Drink, but Don't Be Too Merry

The first discovery I made was that I had a drinking problem.

Before college, I never drank alcohol. Two weeks into college and after a noble fight to resist it, I had my first taste of beer. For the next 22 years, I indulged. I was never a rip-roaring drunk who spent lunch hours at the local bar or nights wandering the streets looking for his car. More typically, I might have a beer or two each night during the week and then several drinks on the weekend nights. Socially, this was acceptable, so I never considered it a problem. But in 2000, between Thanksgiving and New Year's Day, I found myself drinking at least two drinks every day and looking forward to them from the minute I woke up in the morning.

The first indication of a problem was at Thanksgiving when I was watching the movie *Gladiator* with my family and I just fell out of my chair. At first, I thought someone had pushed me. Then I realized that I had had too much to drink to stay upright on my own. In hindsight, it was funny. At the time, it was nauseating.

The next clue came on New Year's Eve, at a party with friends, when I started tripping some kids as they ran around our pool table. I thought it was funny. Their parents did not. A few days later, I ran into a friend who was not even at the party. She said, "I heard *you* had a good time at the party."

Word had spread that I had been drunk. And I thought to myself, "Do I really want to be known as the guy who drinks too much? As the guy who tortures children when he drinks? And we had a party?"

So I quit cold turkey. And it was one of the best life decisions I ever made. Today, ten years later, I feel much better than I did when I was drinking. I don't wake up in the morning with cobwebs in my head, nor do I fall out of chairs. The stupid things I do today are because of my immaturity, not the alcohol. What a nice feeling.

A Rash of Poor Eating

The second major health improvement I made was when I discovered I was allergic to dairy products. It happened purely by accident, when I was talking with a friend, Cheryl Mirabella, who happened to be trained in holistic nutrition. I explained how I had been getting head colds 3-4 times a year and that I had been battling hives for almost ten years without any discernible cause.

Cheryl tracked my eating habits and determined that I was consuming too much dairy, too much caffeine, and too much sugar. So, once again, I quit cold turkey. This was much harder than the alcohol. But I immediately felt better. The hives disappeared and I didn't get a cold for 2½ years.

Today, I eat much healthier than I used to, but I still struggle with sugar and caffeine. I'm a hardcore fan of Cinnabons, Reese's Eggs, and strong coffee. But what I've discovered is that my body functions better when I eat healthy foods, such as vegetables, fruits, and seafood, than when I load up with red meat and sweets.

So, the Do It Well concept kicks in when we consider that our bodies, like our cars, need the right fuel and the right maintenance. I'm not a nutrition expert, nor do I have a degree in fitness. But I know what works for me, and I suspect that these simple techniques will work for you as well.

I hired Cheryl to help me with my diet. I also hired a personal trainer to help me get my fitness plan together. I would suggest others do the same, because most of us don't realize that our diets and exercise are not right for our particular bodies. With a little bit of external expertise, we can make a few simple changes that will have a lasting health impact.

The Well-Fun-Health Process

Good health doesn't have to be miserable or painful. Here are some simple tips that will make a big difference in your long-term health. I'm not a doctor, a nutritionist, or even a health expert. I just know that most experts agree that the following steps lead to a healthier lifestyle. After that is a list of ways to make healthfulness more fun. Since most of us fail because it's no fun, these tips can make us become more successful.

Do It Well

1. When it comes to eating, **fruits and vegetables rule**. Eat more chicken and fish than red meat. And if you have a tough time with cravings, crowd out the bad food with the good food to satisfy your hunger.

2. **Drink plenty of water, and consider taking supplements** like vitamin D and B$_{12}$. Our bodies need the fluid, and the supplements help balance what we might be missing from our diet. Talk to a doctor or a nutritionist to find out the supplements that are best for your body.

3. **Exercise at least three times a week**. You don't have to run a marathon. You just need to get your body moving and your heart pumping. Walking is one of the best things to do, but also consider core strengthening and aerobic activities.

Make It Fun

1. When it comes to diet, try to **make healthy food fun**. A fruit smoothie is a great alternative to a candy bar, and you can experiment with many different flavors. If you cook, you can buy some healthy cookbooks. Make it an adventure rather than a prison sentence and it will be more fun.

2. **Turn exercise into a social event** through team sports, joint activities, and trips to the gym. It's much more fun to be in pain and sweating on the treadmill when someone you know is in pain and sweating too.

3. If you exercise at home, **watch movies, sitcoms, or VH1 while you exercise**. I'd rather sweat to *Braveheart* (which puts my health in the proper perspective) than in silence while I think about how much I hate to exercise. I also use podcasts to keep my mind occupied while I exercise.

Bottom line, if we don't have our health, we're most likely dead. If that's not encouragement enough, do it for the children. I'm not sure what that means, but it always seems to work for fund-raising.

Be healthy. Make the process fun. Our knees and our nephews will thank us. (Get it? Knees and nephews?)

Chapter 8

No One Gets Out Alive

As I've mentioned, I grew up in a small town of 280 people. I knew most of the people in my town and I went to a lot of their funerals. It was the thing we did, out of respect for the person and the family, no matter how well we knew them.

Once, when I was eight years old, I was attending a service at the local funeral home for our deceased neighbor. I was returning from the bathroom, got turned around, and accidentally walked into the wrong room. There, right in front of me was a dead guy. While a dead guy wasn't too surprising for a funeral home, it was terribly surprising for an eight-year-old boy. And what was worse, they had him propped up so that his head jutted out above the top edge of the coffin. It was as if they wanted to give *him* a better view of the room. I turned so fast to get out of the room, I bumped into the sign that read, "Slumber Room 3: Mr. Joseph Thomas."

I didn't slumber well for a month.

Thus began my fascination with death. Not in a morbid, killing-small-animals-with-a-stick way, but in a why-don't-we-ever-talk-about-it way. And the more I thought about it, the more I saw signs of death all around me. I'd notice a hearse right next to me at a stoplight. I'd notice every funeral home in every town I visited. And then for a couple of summers, I mowed cemeteries. I was a death magnet, and I was fascinated with why we, as a society, avoided talking about death.

No One Is Immune

When I was in graduate school, I got my first real taste of a more tragic and personal death. My seven-year-old nephew Allen died of a brain tumor. It was a pretty horrific experience, but even as a 25-year-old, I don't think I fully grasped the impact—especially on my brother and his wife. Now that I have children, I can't imagine what they went through. But they *did* get through it.

After Allen died, my brother and sister-in-law wanted to give their surviving children, a two-year-old daughter and a four-year-old son, the opportunity to discuss their emotional reaction to their brother's death. They chose to read a fantastic book by Leo Buscaglia called *The Fall of Freddy the Leaf.* This book is a metaphorical story about a leaf named Freddy who doesn't want to let go of his tree when fall arrives. In the dialogue between Freddy and one of the wiser leaves, Freddy discovers that letting go is part of the life cycle of a leaf and that he will ultimately fall to the ground, decompose, and nourish the tree for future generations of leaves. The book is a wonderful allegory of life and death. In fact, we typically read this book to members of bereavement groups when I worked in hospice. It was a great tool because it connected with the survivors metaphorically but was also a touching story that allowed them to cry. Crying was healthy for these grieving people, and we loved finding something that led to tears without always focusing on discussions of the person who died. It was covert grief counseling, and Leo Buscaglia was our secret agent.

So, my brother read this same book to his kids. They pulled up chairs in front of the fire and sat there for twenty minutes as he read them the story. By the end, he and his wife were sobbing uncontrollably but both kids were quite calm.

After composing himself, my brother asked his son Wes, "What did you think?"

Wes said, "My feet are hot."

Perfect.

They made a big fuss about trying to get their kids to deal with death, and the kids basically responded by acknowledging that they had dealt with it and now they were on to more important things—like the heat of the fire on their feet.

My time in hospice care taught me that death is real, that it will happen to all of us, and that most of us are not prepared for it. Elisabeth Kübler-Ross was the first to make the process of dying mainstream. Her five stages of dying include denial, anger, bargaining, depression, and acceptance. As she so eloquently explained, there are several steps in the process before we get to acceptance. And from my experience, very few people really get to acceptance. Those who did lived an accepting life already and were typically in a place where death was simply one more experience in their repertoire. But most of us cling to denial and are then shocked when we actually have to face death.

So how can we approach the process of aging and death better, and is it possible to make it more fun? Yes on both counts. In fact, "funeral" starts with "f-u-n."

Face It, We All Die

First of all, we're supposed to get old. As someone once said, "Getting old isn't the problem. It's when we stop getting old that the trouble starts."

So true. Our bodies get older, we get sick, and we die. Hopefully in that order. So each step along the way requires an ability to accept what *is* rather than wish for what is no more. I refer you to Chapter 2 if this is still unclear.

In 2002, my friend Roz Trieber was diagnosed with breast cancer. I mentioned her in a previous chapter. In typical Roz fashion, she approached this challenge as just one more bump, so to speak, on the road of life. She told the surgeon she didn't have time for cancer because she had too much to do. And when she was being prepped for her lumpectomy, the nurse raised the sheet to find two clown noses strategically placed on each breast. It broke the tension for Roz and kept everyone's spirits high.

Five years later, Roz was again diagnosed with cancer. This time it was in her pancreas. She said she was "numb" after hearing the diagnosis, but then she quickly regressed (in a good way) to her normal state of a playful mind. While in the hospital, she handed out clown noses and copies of her book, *Live Life Laughing,* to the other patients.

She said, "Helping other people made me feel better."

That's the extraordinary attitude of Roz Trieber. She was simply joy personified.

After a difficult round of treatments for her cancer, Roz's condition improved for a year or so. Then, in February of 2009, the cancer returned. And this time, it had spread throughout her abdomen. She tried eight days of radiation but told her physician that the treatment was killing her faster than the cancer. She stopped the radiation and opted for hospice care instead. She wanted a better quality of life for whatever time she had left.

Most of us would have probably thrown in the towel at that point. But Roz continued to find ways to be positive and have a positive impact on those around her. One day she wore a clown nose (this time on her nose) to her doctor's appointment. Other patients asked where they could get one. Roz proudly replied, "From me."

She sold seven of them.

In 2009, Roz died. Her funeral was a celebration of everything she stood for. It was sad but, at the same time, funny and inspirational. I think Roz would have wanted it that way. She did it well and made it fun.

Dying for a Good Laugh

My friend Theo Androus's dad was quite a character. He also had a number of health challenges, including diabetes. As his surgeon was discussing the likelihood that his leg would need to be amputated, Theo's dad asked if he could have his leg back after the surgery. The surprised surgeon asked why.

He said, "Because I want to bury it under my tombstone with a sign that says, 'The Rest Is Yet to Come.'"

That was the way Theo's dad approached life—up front and with a touch of humor.

When his dad died, Theo called me to let me know. After I offered my condolences, Theo said, "I'd like your advice about something. Since you worked in hospice care and you have some experience with humor, I want to run an idea past you. There are certain family members who had a really close relationship with my dad. A big part of their relationship was humor. So, I'd like to have some fun with them at the viewing. I'd like to put the speaker portion of a baby monitor in the coffin. Then, when these folks are viewing his body, I want to talk to them. (Long pause.) What do you think?"

I thought for a minute and said, "Dude, you will not find a greater proponent of humor than me. But you're on your own on this one!"

I didn't know how to advise him. On the one hand, it could be hysterical. On the other hand, it could be disastrous. I didn't want to be responsible for the chance of disastrous.

I apologized for not giving him advice but told him I'd love to know what he ultimately decided to do.

Two weeks later I got the call.

Theo said, "Well, we did it."

He described how they only tried it with a few people who they knew would appreciate it. For instance, one cousin named Johnny was viewing the body. Theo's dad and Johnny had been very close and they had shared a lot of humor with each other. While Johnny was standing over the coffin, in a very poignant moment, he heard this: "Hey, Johnny. (Pause.) You're next."

Johnny burst out laughing.

He loved it.

And I suspect that the reason he loved it was that it connected him with the essence of this very special relationship. Theo knew that. And he took advantage of a very unusual idea to create that connection. Theo was braver than I would have been.

Theo's dad embraced life, but, at the same time, he did not avoid death. After his death, Theo carried the same torch. They did life well. They did death well. And in both, they had fun along the way.

The Well-Fun-Death Process

You may wonder why the chapter on death isn't at the end of the book. It's because a good death begins with a good life. The best thing we can do in life is to understand that we will eventually face death. It's about planning our death by planning our life. If we're going on vacation, we don't simply get in the car unprepared. No. We pack, we map out the trip, we tell people we'll be gone, and we prepare. The same is true with life. We should plan it as if we know the end result. We don't waste our time, but we don't ignore the clock, either. There is a limit to our lives. That's reality.

Here are a few tips to prepare for the end of life ... whether we're at the beginning, the middle, or the end:

Do It Well

1. **Never take anything for granted**. Let's be appreciative for all that we have—our health, our significant other, our family, our job, our house, our pets, our collection of decorative spoons from all 50 states, etc. It's all temporary and to enjoy it is to value it.

2. **Say it now**. It's important to those around us how much we appreciate them. Now is always better than later. Unless we are going to tell them that we like how much weight they've gained. That can weight (get it?).

3. **Imagine how you want to be remembered**. By seeing what the end of the game looks like, we tend to play the game better. We should be specific and do what we need to do to achieve the end result.

Make It Fun

1. Keep this mantra in mind: **"Face each day as if it were your last,** because one day you'll be right." Not only is it true, it's funny.

2. Remember that **humor can happen anywhere**—even in times of death and grief. Most funerals contain funny memories about the person that died. This is because we need to remember the good as well as the sad. We shouldn't feel guilty for enjoying a bit of humor when we're in the presence of death.

3. **Life is full of joy and tragedy**. We must experience both to appreciate either. When we're experiencing our own illness

and death or the illness and death of someone else, we will have a tendency to see the tragedy of the situation. If we try to see the joy as well, we can make the journey of life richer.

The game plan for death (and life) is this: Do it well. Do it now. And, for goodness' sake, make it fun.

Section 2:

Playing Well with Others

Chapter 9

Say What?

Most of us have the ability to speak. Most of us have the ability to hear. Having both speaking and hearing should make communication pretty seamless.

And yet it is still quite difficult, because most of us don't fully understand the process.

When I was in college, I was with a group of guys returning to our dorm one evening after dinner. One of the guys, Bill, had brought back two grapefruits that he'd snatched from the dessert table in the cafeteria. He was bouncing them off the back of Dan's head. Somewhat annoyed, Dan smacked one of the grapefruits to the ground and it split open.

Bill said, "Hey, I was going to eat that."

Dan took off running while Bill picked up the split grapefruit and ran after him. Halfway up the dorm stairs, Bill threw the grapefruit and hit Dan square in face.

Dan grabbed Bill and was just about to punch him when I intervened. I pulled them apart and said, "Dan, settle down. Bill was just having fun. But because you got hit in the face, you're embarrassed and your reacting to the embarrassment rather than really wanting to hurt Bill."

I'm not sure where that analysis came from. I was like a young Sigmund Freud without my slip. Or Dr. Phil with hair. It just came out of me as an intuitive observation and without any forethought whatsoever.

Dan looked at me and said, "You know, you're right. Sorry, Bill. I overreacted."

And that was that. The rest of the evening was uneventful.

I'm not sure I have ever been that direct with anyone. At the time, it just seemed right, but now I realize it was a very bold move and that I could have been punched in the face, with a grapefruit!

What's the Problem?

I wonder if that fear is what keeps us from communicating effectively as adults: the fear of being punched in the face. While we may not be afraid of literally being punched in the face, we *are* afraid of being rejected, ridiculed, or ignored. Essentially, we're afraid of being punched in the ego. So we avoid honest communication because we have an anticipatory fear of what might happen. It's not necessarily the reality, but it *is* the reality we create in our head, forcing us to avoid communicating directly and honestly.

By naming the *real* reality in the grapefruit incident, I inadvertently took the imaginary realities out of the situation and brought everyone to the actual reality of the moment. That way, we could be our true selves rather than trying to be something we were not, such as cool, tough guys who never make mistakes. Believe me, I did not know what I was doing at the time, but in hindsight, I now see the power of words, the power of reality, and the power of effective communication.

But ineffective communication happens all the time. Sometimes it's funny. Sometimes it's disastrous.

One night at dinner, I was explaining the difference between the North and the South to my 11-year-old son, Ryan. Since I grew up in southwest Virginia and my wife, Wendy, grew up on Long Island, I was highlighting our different upbringings.

I said, "When I was in high school, I went to Patrick Henry High School in Glade Spring, Virginia. We were the Patrick Henry Rebels. There was a huge Confederate flag painted on the side of our football stadium, and every time the football team scored a touchdown, the band played 'Dixie.'"

I looked at Ryan and said, "That's not appropriate, and thank goodness, they don't do that anymore."

Ryan had this very pained expression on his face. He looked at me and said, "Dad, you went to high school during the Civil War?"

Apparently, regardless of the best efforts of great educators, some children are "left behind."

We laughed hysterically at his comment, and it didn't take him long to realize his mistake. But a simple story led to a significant miscommunication. Can you imagine how often this happens during our work day? Or in our relationships?

There's an exercise I do in my workshops in which I show an audience member a photo of a Norman Rockwell painting. Then, that person has one minute to describe the painting to another member of the audience. At that point, the description is passed in turn to four other people, but each person now describing the painting has not seen the painting. It's a variation on the old game called Gossip, and you would be amazed by the variation that occurs between the first description and the last.

During one session, a person described the "green grass" in the painting. The next person referred to it as "marijuana"!

Another time, a man said that there was a father in the scene but the mother was "not in the picture." The next person, who grew up in a single-parent family, said, "There is a single-parent family in the scene."

What shocks me about this exercise is that it's not a difficult photo to describe. But most people get so caught up in the details, they ignore what the painting represents. If, instead, they described the meaning of the scene, the receiver would hear much more than just the details. They would hear a story that would be much more memorable to describe to the next person.

In our own daily communications, we may think we've been perfectly clear with someone and yet they hear something totally different. And usually it's because we didn't confirm what they heard and we both assume we're on the same page.

The Well-Fun-Communication Process

The formula for good communication is quite simple and only requires three steps. Consider the following to enhance your communication effectiveness.

Do It Well

1. The first thing to consider when you communicate is **what you intend to say**. Once we know what we want to say, half the battle is over. But here's the thing: sometimes what we intend to say comes out poorly because we are not clear and honest. "I love you" is very clear. "I like to hang out with you" may mean the same thing, but it's not as clear.

2. The second step in good communication is **what you say and how you say it**. Even if you have bad news to tell someone and you don't want to upset them, by watering down your comments or misleading them because you're not clear,

you won't convey what you intend. Be clear and honest but with a great deal of care.

3. The final step in effective communication is **what the other person heard you say**. While we may think we're clear, the other person may not have understood what we intended. As a rule, it's a good idea to ask for feedback so you know what the other person heard. Then, start the entire process over again for the next thing you want to communicate.

Here's an example from real life. As a manager, I had to tell an employee that I had received complaints from staff about his body odor. Now, this is one of the most awkward situations a manager can have. I was afraid it would embarrass the employee, and yet I needed him to do something about it. So here's how the conversation went:

I said, "Al, I need to discuss something with you. I must say that it is an uncomfortable conversation to have and I want you to know that I appreciate you very much and don't mean to make you feel awkward. That being said, I have received several concerns about your body odor. Some of the folks who work with you feel that it needs to be addressed so that it does not affect your work with other staff and patients. I'm sorry to have to bring this to your attention."

Al said, "Thank you for letting me know. It is uncomfortable, but I appreciate the way you handled it."

I said, "So you understand that you need to address this?"

He said, "Yes."

I suggested he use a different soap or deodorant and he agreed to try.

Then I said, "I know this situation stinks but it is what it is."

OK, I didn't say that last part, and while it would have been funny, it would have also been insensitive. But we'll get to the fun in communication later.

So if I look back at the formula, I knew what I had to convey to Al, and then I conveyed it with full consideration of how it might impact him. Then, I circled back to make sure he understood what I said. If you hit these three touch points for communication, you will eliminate most miscommunication.

Make It Fun

Once we have the basics of communication mastered, we will realize that humor is a great communication tool that can make the process both easier and more fun.

1. Be willing to **use humor in communications**. The less self-protective we are and the more willing we are to make fun of ourselves, the easier it is to communicate effectively. I read in Allen Klein's book *The Healing Power of Humor,* a story about a woman who got pulled over for speeding. When the cop came to her window, she gave him a "Get Out of Jail Free" card from *Monopoly*. Great use of humor.

2. Be willing to **laugh at your mistakes**. When we miscommunicate, we can't get consumed by our ego telling us that we need to cover up our mistake. Instead, we can embrace it. It not only makes communication easier, but also makes us a great role model for others.

3. **Prepare for difficult communication with humor**. Sharing a joke or a cartoon with someone can loosen up the atmosphere so that you can then get to the business of the difficult communication.

Good communication leads to better relationships.

Chapter 10

Is Your BFF AWOL?

I remember the first time I saw "BFF," I couldn't help thinking, well, BFD. If you don't know what that is, look it up. And don't get mad at me for writing it here. I just use foul language through acronyms, not through the real words.

I've never called anyone my BFF, nor have I ever had a best, best, bestest friend, unless I count my wife, Wendy, who I suppose is really my BWF. But she is obligated to be my best friend, so I don't really have to worry about doing friend things with her because, basically, we sleep together and that's about the closest friend thing I can do.

With real friends, though, it's different. We have to be purposeful about our relationships or else they die (the relationships, not the friends).

When I was in a kid, I had several close friends. I still keep in touch with a couple of them through Christmas cards, social media, and sometimes when I visit my mom. These friends are like family. They're friends because they were just always there—even if we have very little in common today.

Then, there are my friends from high school or college who stay in touch more regularly. These are the guys who still see the world as I do and share common interests. We thoroughly enjoy getting together at class reunions or sporting events, or when one of us passes a major life milestone. I maintain these friendships a bit more than the family-esque friends.

You Gotta Have Friends

When I turned 30, it occurred to me that I didn't really have a best friend, other than my BWF. I think this happens more with men, although I have no data to back it up. We men tend to enjoy each other's company, but we don't strategically manage friendships. They either happen by proximity through work or sports, or they don't. I didn't have a close friend whom I could talk to or confide in—that is, if I had something to confide. So I told Wendy that I was going to be more purposeful in pursuing my male friendships (she would not have been happy if I wanted to be more purposeful in my female relationships). Two things happened to help me accomplish that goal.

First, Wendy and I were part of a small group in our church. Our group contained six couples, all about the same age, who met twice a month to pray for one another, socialize, and do a Bible study or discuss a spiritually focused book. Since we attended a large church, our small group became our social and spiritual connection to the church, and the other couples became our good friends. We've shared childbirths, deaths of parents, job losses, and other life events with these people, and we've gotten to know them very well. But I still didn't have a single best friend in the group whom I talked to regularly or with whom I would share the more intimate details of my life.

Shortly after we joined the group, I came up with an idea for the men to get together on a regular basis, in hopes of building stronger friendships. Since men typically don't get together for dinner just to talk about their lacking relationships, I figured we needed something purposeful to bring us together. So I created JAM (Joint Activities for Men) Sessions. Six times each year, on a Saturday morning, all six men would show up at one of our houses and spend 4 to 5 hours doing all those odd jobs we could never get done. We mulched, we painted, we hung cabinets, and we enjoyed each other's company. As a result, once a year, each of us got the benefit of a small work crew to do whatever we needed done.

It was a fantastic way to build relationships and be productive at the same time. Unfortunately, when we all started having children, we had a very hard time finding even *one* Saturday during the year when we were all available to work. So, the JAM Sessions fizzled out. Yet it is one of the fondest memories I have of the friendships I've developed.

From that same small group, a golf trip developed. All of the men in our group played golf. Some even played well. So, one day Rick Webster sent us an invitation to go to Kiawah Island Golf Resort for three days of golf, using a discounted package he got from American Express for January—since, of course, January is an iffy time to play golf in South Carolina. Two guys couldn't go, so Mark Haus, Rick, and I went. It was wonderful. We shared a villa and played as much golf as we could in three days. It was male bonding heaven.

A year or so later, our associate pastor, Bob Griffin, and his wife joined our small group. Bob was a scratch golfer in high school, so he fit right in with our Kiawah group. But Bob, being a pastoresque guy, also saw our outing as a way to bring other men in the church together. So he eventually developed our trip into an all-church golf outing that grew to 28 golfers. It's one of the many ministries in our church, and it all started from a need a men had to get together and to build relationships.

We all need relationships outside of our families. While our closest relationships are our partners or spouses, we also need to have an "outsider" with whom we can discuss our work, our relationships, and our life challenges. It gives us support from an objective person and allows us to develop what the Bible calls an agape type of love.

It's not family and it's not romantic, but it's still close and is usually unconditional.

The challenge is to find these friends and then, once we find them, to maintain and nurture the relationships.

Seek and Ye Shall Find

I've owned my business for 15 years. As a speaker and author, I have a home office but I also travel a lot. It can be a lonely job. My clients are not usually close friends, so I need other ways to connect with people on a more intimate level. Two friendships developed from this need for a business relationship.

The first came as a result of my membership in the National Speakers Association (NSA). This is the professional organization for people who speak for a living. I've been a member for most of my career and have developed some lasting friendships with a number of my speaker colleagues. One of those speakers, David Glickman, is not only a very close friend but also my business partner at Funnier Speeches, LLC (www.FunnierSpeeches.com). We met at NSA where, because we are both humorists, we had gravitated toward each other. As we got to know each other better, we not only respected each other for our humor skills but also for our shared values and work ethics. Ironically, David is Jewish and I am Christian. This difference in our faith has added a unique dimension and depth to our relationship. In fact, one of my favorite lines from David came when I asked him when he was getting back to his office after a December cruise. He said, "We're coming back on Christmas Day, or, as we call it, Thursday." Very funny.

David and I talk almost every week, and we have supported each other through a number of life challenges, including the deaths of our fathers. Our friendship is solid. We even have a clause in our business plan that says that we will dissolve the business before we dissolve our friendship.

The second important relationship I developed arose from my

church and then spread to my business. I had been meeting regularly with Bob Griffin as both a friend and a Christian accountability partner, but he moved to Pennsylvania and we were not able to maintain our meetings. After Bob moved, a very good speaker friend and also a Christian, Mike Rayburn, moved near me and asked if I was interested in a similar accountability relationship. He suggested that we meet regularly as a way to help each other maintain our commitments to our faith, our families, our work, etc. We met twice a month over coffee and developed a very solid relationship. Unfortunately, Mike moved to Las Vegas and while we tried to maintain the relationship over the phone, it proved to be too difficult. We are still very close friends but we do not have the benefit of meeting regularly.

Once I experienced that type of friendship, I began to search for a similar situation—and it was right there in front of me. I had met one of our associate pastors, David Jordan-Haas, at a men's retreat. I truly appreciated his heart and his spiritual perspective on men and faith. After my motorcycle accident, he visited me and offered some very comforting words as I struggled with the existential questions that arise after a life-altering experience (Why did I live? What should my next motorcycle be?).

So, assuming that we had other things in common, I approached David and asked if he would be interested in developing a spiritual friendship. He was delighted and we've been meeting ever since. We go to the local Starbucks and talk about whatever is on our hearts. We've supported each other with issues of faith, family, and health. In fact, we had our colonoscopies just a few weeks apart. Talk about bonding! But I wouldn't trade this friendship for anything. Our meetings are like an agape latte!

The Well-Fun-Friendship Process

So, where do we find our friendships and how do we make them fun? That's a good question. Usually, the prospects are right in front of us. We just don't pursue them purposefully. If we look in our jobs, our faith communities, our civic organizations, or other groups in which we belong, there is most likely someone who shares our interests and who could be that BFF. Or at least a BFFAYOS (Best Friend For A Year Or So). We make a list of our prospects, and when the time is right, approach them to do something together. We don't have to ask them to move in with us. First, we can have coffee, play golf, or work on our lawnmower together and determine if there is the basis for a friendship. If there is, we might consider being more purposeful in the relationship. That's when we Friend Them well and Friend Them Fun, to borrow from Facebook lingo.

Here are some suggestions for nurturing those close friendships in our life:

Do it Well

1. Remember to **use good listening skills**. Listening is key to building a relationship, because one of the things we appreciate about our friends is that they listen to us. Are you listening to me? I said listening is important to friendships. Probably the most important quality.

2. **Schedule regular time together** for coffee, a meal, or a joint activity. If you neglect the time together, you won't be able to move forward in your friendship. It's also important to acknowledge special events like birthdays, anniversaries, colonoscopies, etc. You can call, e-mail, or send a card to let your friends know you're thinking of them.

3. **Use your friends as advisors,** and don't be afraid to call on them when you need advice or support. Real friends don't appreciate knowing that you had a problem and didn't talk to them about it.

Make It Fun

1. As a golfer, one of my favorite things to do with my friends is to play golf. It's an activity where there is a goal (score low) but there is also a process (enjoying each other's company and making fun of their shots). **Participating in joint activities** such as sports, shopping, or entertainment events together are all fun ways to build friendships.

2. **Make communicating with each other fun**. Whenever David Glickman and I call each other, we always answer the phone in a funny way. Whatever is going on with one of us, the other tries to incorporate that in the way we answer the phone. It reminds me of the practical jokes that I enjoyed when I worked at the psychiatric hospital. You just never know what's going to happen, and it's funny.

3. **Send fun gifts and cards**. Every once in a while, I'll get a perfect gift from a friend for no reason. It might be a Starbucks card, a book on humor, or a small motorcycle sculpted out of scrap metal. We should think of our friends and share a fun gift now and then.

Friends are critical to our well-fun-ness. As James Taylor sang, "You've got a friend" (somewhere). It's just up to us to find him or her.

Chapter 11

The Mine Is the
First Thing to Go

One of the most significant relationships we'll ever have is with our partner or spouse. And yet we're often surprised when we realize that it is a significant change in lifestyle that requires that we go from a *me* mentality to a *we* mentality. These changes in priority are very hard to manage, especially for those of us who are narcissistically self-centered, but we must adjust if we're going to have a solid and fun relationship.

I didn't date much in high school. Big surprise. You see, I was not a very confident person, and I feared rejection and avoided it like the plague. I did, however, by some miracle, date three girls in high school, each for a short period of time. While I enjoyed their company, thought each was attractive, and fantasized about the possibility of kissing them, which, by the way, I had no idea how to approach, I must admit that there was one quality that really got under my skin. These girls did not have the same sense of humor that I had. I'd go so far as to say that they didn't have *any* sense of humor.

If I was on a date, I might tell my date the most recent joke I'd heard by saying, "So, this hot dog walked into a bar and the bartender said, 'I'm sorry, we don't serve food here.'"

I know. Hilarious, right?

And yet, I'd look over at my date and she'd have this contorted frown on her face and a vacant look in her eyes.

I'd say, "What's wrong?"

She'd say, "I didn't get it."

Sadly, I would then attempt to explain the joke. Which I know now is against the humor policies of the universe.

"So, you see, the hot dog is food. So the bartender is using a play on words by saying they don't serve food to *eat* there. Like some bars don't. Serve food, that is. But not referring to the hot dog. Which is also food. But in this case, not food that you'd eat. At least in that situation. In the bar. See how funny that is?"

Inevitably, my date would give me a polite smile, turn away, and say, "Oh."

Ugh.

This was an even more insidious type of rejection than simple date rejection. She was rejecting my humor, which was the essence of who I was. It cut me right to the core, and what's worse, I had to abandon my humor and return to the inane conversation about who was dating whom and what happened on the most recent episode of *Petticoat Junction*. It was depressing.

It happened so much, I was convinced that I would go through life having to explain every joke to every date I had. I envisioned being married to someone for the rest of my life who hated *Monty Python* and who didn't understand the intricate humor of a Steve Martin's *Happy Feet* routine. I was not looking at a happy future.

In my first year at the University of Virginia, I started dating Wendy Colclough, an intelligent and attractive New Yorker who, when we first met, was not put off by my white bibbed overalls and shirtless (chiseled) physique. She would eventually, and luckily, I might add, become my wife. On our second date, I told her a joke. I said, "This three-legged dog walked into an old west saloon and said, 'I'm looking for the man who shot my pa.'"

Proud of my perfect delivery of the punch line, I looked at Wendy and immediately recognized that familiar contorted frown from every date I had in high school. I was deflated. I felt the light drain out of my heart. And with a voice of defeat, I said, "I guess you didn't get the joke."

My valedictorian, future wife looked at me and said, "Oh, I *got* it. I just didn't think it was very funny."

A surge of adrenaline shot through my body. Could there be a woman who not only appreciated humor, but frowned upon bad humor? I never knew one existed, and in that moment, I realized that this one was on a date with me. The rest, as they say, was history. And for what it's worth, I was the lucky one.

I Do, I Did, and I Will

I usually share the previous story when Wendy and I lead a session in the pre-marriage seminar series at our church. Our topic focuses on the differences in people's expectations in relationships. We tend to go into a marriage looking for our own benefits and fail to realize that the other person may have different expectations for the relationship. We also cover the principles from the outstanding book by Gary Chapman called *The Five Love Languages,* in which Chapman points out that our way of expressing love to our spouse is usually based on what we want rather than what our spouse wants.

To me, this is the ultimate challenge of marriage. I mean, I got married because I loved Wendy and I loved the way she made me feel. But the true goal of a successful marriage or long-term relationship is to meet the needs of our spouse rather than just getting our own needs met. But that's really tough. Luckily, I married Wendy, who, in my humble opinion, is the best wife in the world. She puts herself second. Not in a martyr, look-at-all-I'm-sacrificing way, but by always seeing the needs of the family before her own. And she does this on top of a full-time job at IBM. Did I score a winner or what?

In *The Road Less Traveled*, Scott Peck suggests that our goal in a marriage is to provide enough love and support to enable our spouse to reach his or her greatest potential.

Imagine that.

He's saying that the goal in *my* marriage is not to get the most out of Wendy so that I feel loved and successful but instead to help her succeed in her work, in her life, and in her family. For most of us, that concept is so hard, it's almost abstract. How do we make that happen when there aren't a lot of good role models out there to teach us?

First, we have to understand that we are similar but different. We obviously have things in common that attracted us to each other, but we are also very different people who have different perspectives and different expectations. For instance, I'm a bit OCD, as I've mentioned. Wendy is not.

While my OCD may drive *her* crazy, it really works for me. For one, I'll never miss a bill payment. I've got a great system using file folders for each day of the month. I simply put my bills in a folder one week before they're due and voilà, no late fees. Of course in order for this system to work, I have to check the folders every day. Unfortunately, I sometimes forget to do that. So, I developed another system using a note that says "Check bill folder," which reminds me to put an entry on my computerized to-do list to check the folder. That way, I can transfer that reminder to my daily handwritten to-do list and voilà, I never miss a bill payment. As you can see, it's a great system.

Another benefit is that I don't tolerate clutter. Everything has its place.

When I need the remote control, I know where it is.

If I use the last three squares of toilet paper (which I have systematically determined is the proper average usage amount), another roll is right there.

When I'm fixing a tasty gourmet meal, I know exactly where to find every ingredient, unless Wendy put away the groceries and placed the teriyaki marinade with the "m" foods instead of the "t" foods, where it belongs. In that case, I might not be able to find it and have to substitute Worcestershire for teriyaki, which I think we can all agree is a total disaster.

Finally, my order disorder means that my house will never burn down because I left the iron on. When we go on trips I not only turn the iron off, I make sure the light timer is on, none of the toilets are running, and the pillows are positioned properly on the couch according to thread count. Then, I double-check that I've checked everything a couple of times, since I never can be too sure.

None of those details really matter to Wendy. If a can of soup is on the cereal shelf, she can live with that. If she can't find the soup, she just buys another can. I, on the other hand, will empty the shelves looking for the bloody can of soup that I *know* is there. And this is where the problems in most marriages arise. People believe their way is not just different, it's right. And even though it is, in my case, it's probably unreasonable for me to impose that belief on her, since she embraces another, albeit wrong, perspective.

Essentially, marriage is a partnership. It's similar to how business partners work together for the good of the company. Spouses must do the same for the marriage. If we're not willing to meet halfway, then we'll never really benefit from the richness that the relationship has to offer.

The Well-Fun-Marriage Process

In marriage, we must love together and we must laugh together. That requires that we spend as much time on what makes our spouse feel loved and what makes *her* laugh as we do on what makes us feel loved and what makes us laugh. So, here are some tips to make your marriages adept:

Do It Well

1. **Regularly write down the things that you love about your spouse**. What attracted you to him or her in the first place? Was it his quick wit? Was it her intellect? Was it his buns of steel? Make a list and keep it where you can refer to it. This is your fire alarm to bring you back to safety when things get tough.

2. **Make a list of the things that you do differently from your spouse** or significant other. In other words, the things that get under your skin. Next to each of these items, in a second column, describe why he or she might see these things differently. Next to that column, ask yourself, "So what?" In the big scheme of things, does it really matter?

3. **Set aside some time to ask your spouse what things you do that make him or her feel loved**. Once you have your list of items, you can just do it!

Make It Fun

1. A couple that laughs together lasts together. **You need to find times to laugh** with your spouses. Whether it's watching a funny movie, telling each other jokes, or reminiscing about all the funny things your kids did, a regular chuckling session can help you avoid a counseling session.

2. **Think about the fun things that you like to do, that your spouse likes to do, and that you like to do together.** Take time to schedule fun activities every month. Don't wait for them to happen spontaneously, but make them happen.

3. **Schedule date nights on a regular basis.** These can be fun times to catch up on your relationship and to strengthen your marriage. You can use the time to really get to the heart of your marriage.

A marriage that seeks to reach its greatest potential while enjoying the journey is a marriage that will last beyond all of the statistics that suggest it's not going to succeed.

We can be our own statistic. Marry well and marry fun.

Chapter 12

Because I Said So

When I was in fourth grade, I recall having assigned seats that changed throughout the year. For a particular time, I sat behind a guy named Chris. He was a large boy, his clothes were worn, and he was not a stellar student. He came from a blue-collar family, as did most of the kids in my community, and he was quiet. I don't remember either liking Chris or disliking him. We played in different circles and only occasionally interacted.

One day, Chris came to school walking rather gingerly. I don't remember how it came up in the conversation, but I remember him saying that his father had "beat him with the branch of a rose bush" the night before. I was stunned and didn't know what to say. And the saddest thing to me was that this was probably not the first time this had happened to Chris. Most likely, it was the way that his parents were raised, the way their parents were raised, and so on.

Many years later, I worked for the Division of Child Protection at Children's National Medical Center in Washington, DC. I saw a lot of Chrises in that job, and it was there that I understood what child abuse looked like. Our division encountered 40 to 50 new cases of abuse per week, and the vast majority were simply a continuation of parenting styles that were handed down from generation to generation.

Until I had children, I couldn't understand how anyone could be abusive to their children. After I had kids, I understood. No, don't get me wrong. I'm not abusive, nor do I condone abuse, or even corporal punishment for that matter. I just understand how it can happen.

When most of us become parents, we figure that if everyone else can do it, so can we. But the only role models we have are our own parents. My parents weren't perfect. My wife's parents weren't perfect. None of our parents were perfect. Clearly, we have a flaw in the system in that our parents, the only role models we have, are not really there to provide mentoring. They got into the job the same way we did—and they did the best that they could. So, knowing we don't always have good role models, how do we learn to be good parents? Just like everything else in this book, we seek ways to do it well and make it fun.

We must not assume that we'll figure it out on our own.

My Kids' Father Isn't Perfect Either

I was a terrible parent when my children were infants. I was sleep deprived and had a very hard time dealing with the fact that I couldn't convince them to stop crying at 3:00 a.m. It was in those moments when I'd lose my cool and yell at my small children—as if a verbal Ambien® would put them to sleep. In those instances, I realized how someone with less impulse control could abuse their power.

When my daughter Caitlin was born, Wendy took four months off from work while I, the typical male, continued to work. Wendy would get up with Caitlin on weeknights and I would get up on the weekend nights. But when Wendy went back to work, we ignored the tradition of mothers attending to their children and alternated nights. Some nights Caitlin would cry at 4:00 a.m., and we were both awake but pretended not to hear her. We figured if we could outlast the other, we wouldn't have to get up—no matter whose turn it was. We would lay there perfectly still, barely breathing, while trying to endure a screaming child who usually just needed a pacifier. That's when I discovered that yoga helped me slow down my breaths so I could outlast Wendy.

As our children got older, the challenges changed. We were no longer changing diapers but counseling them on how to get along with classmates. Or consoling them when they didn't make the junior varsity basketball team or the varsity lacrosse team. We supported them when prom dates fell through and when they failed their first driver's test (because they didn't think they needed to read the manual, by the way). But all along, we were figuring it out as we went because there was not a real how-to manual.

But let me make this very important point. Figuring it out as we go does not mean taking it for granted. Wendy and I had lots of hard discussions, sought advice from friends *and* professionals, and read countless articles and books to help us figure it out. We tried hard to do it well, especially the first time around.

Know Your Strengths . . . and Your Not-So-Strengths

There are certain aspects of parenting for which I'm not skilled. For instance, I'm not a homework guy. Wendy is the homework guy, uh, gal. I tried it a few times and told my kids the wrong answers. That's not good, especially during the parent-teacher conferences when we're trying to explain a low grade in physics.

I am creative, though. Unfortunately, most kids don't appreciate the value of creativity until after they leave home and no longer seek their parents' advice.

For years, I tried to convince my kids that when they did a

class presentation or wrote an essay, they should add some humor. I explained that humor would make any presentation better. For instance, in sixth grade, my son Ryan had to do an oral report about his favorite animal. The animal he chose was the cheetah. So, wanting to help him get a better grade and to demonstrate my humor aptitude, I told him that he should include this hilariously crafted line in his report: "The cheetah's favorite food is Cheetos, and they're also known for being terrible cheetahs on tests. Just kidding."

Ryan wouldn't do it. He said he was afraid he would get in trouble if he tried to be funny. Oh, the tragedy of it all. I just couldn't understand how any teacher would penalize him for such a great line.

Caitlin was the same way. She continually refused to use humor in her presentations and essays. Until, that is, she was working on her senior English project in high school and she needed a clever headline for her article. Then, she came to me.

By the way, she got an A. I'm just saying.

And as a side note, when my children applied to the University of Virginia, they had to write a short essay on their favorite word. Caitlin chose "procrastination" and Ryan chose "indecisive." Both essays were parodies. I was so proud.

Good parenting requires that we know our strengths as well as our not-so-strengths (vocabulary is not one of my strengths). Our spouses or partners can fill in the gaps so that we don't have to know everything or do it all. Where Wendy shines is often where I need help. I'm glad to let her help with the homework while I focus my parenting on cheetah jokes.

The Well-Fun-Parenting Process

When it comes to doing parenting well and making it fun, I have a few simple suggestions. I should defer to Wendy on this one, but I'm afraid she doesn't have time to contribute to my book because she's busy helping Ryan with his homework. Here are a few things that will help you to be better parents and to have more fun in the role:

Do It Well

1. **See parenting as a partnership**. If you're married or have a life partner, you should approach parenting as team. You can support each other and make decisions regarding the children together. If you're a single parent, you can find a friend or relative that can serve as your sounding board. Don't go it alone.

2. **Be interested in your children's lives,** but don't be their best friends. The best way to stay connected to your children is to understand their world (music, technology, school, etc.), but to clearly maintain your role as the parent. I listen to contemporary music because it gives me something in common with my kids. I just don't dance to it. That's counterproductive.

3. **Do things together**. In our family we have almost every meal together (both at home and out). We use this time together to build our family relationships. If we start this early, it will become a norm, whereas if we had created separateness early, that would have become the norm.

Make It Fun

1. **Recreate together**. That doesn't sound right. What I mean is to enjoy recreation together. Share in fun activities like sports, movies, games, vacations, etc. The more you do this, the more you'll create fun family traditions.

2. Similarly, **traditions are a great way to develop fun activities** that involve the entire family. We always go to the same restaurant the night before school starts each fall. Our kids look forward to a fun evening out because it is the family tradition.

3. **Write down the funny things your kids say and do.** This gives you an endless supply of material to share with your parent friends, and your kids will love to look at these notes as they get older.

Parenting is one of the hardest jobs we'll ever have. That's why we need to take it seriously but also make it fun. Overall, we must love our children regardless of what they do. We can correct behavior, but we will have a hard time regaining the affection of a child who has come to feel unloved. Good parenting is an investment in the future that will pay more than we realize.

Chapter 13

Ask Not What We Can Do for Others but What They Can Do for Us

C ollege is the ultimate networking environment. I arrived at college not knowing anyone and then had to spend the next four years of my life with these people. I had to figure out how to make friends. Since I was immediately thrust into a dorm environment, my "dormmates" became the first and easiest source of friends. But over time, I realized that proximity was not the best measure of compatibility. Ultimately, my closest friends came from activities I shared with others such as my fraternity, the band, and the guys who dated my girlfriend's housemates.

But there was also the problem of getting to know professors. With classes of 400 students, the professors (and the other students) were not likely to know me or even recognize me. This huge class size made me feel isolated and wonder if my professors had any personal investment in my success.

When I went to grad school in social work, I decided to approach the relationships with my professors differently. Class sizes were smaller and the atmosphere was much less overwhelming than it was in the undergraduate premed weeding-out classes, so there was a greater opportunity to build relationships. I was determined to be known by every professor I had and to get to know my classmates better as well.

When it comes to connecting with others, whether in business or our personal lives, the most important goal is this: Be memorable—in a good way.

At the beginning of every class in grad school, the professor asked each of us to introduce ourselves and tell the class something interesting about our background. While most students chose to discuss their work experience, birthplace, or some grandiose goal of saving the world through social work, I took another route. This was my opportunity to be memorable. So, I would say something like, "My name is Ron Culberson. I got my undergraduate degree at *the* University of Virginia and I'm not only reasonably attractive (and chiseled), I'm one of the nicest people you will ever meet. Oh yeah, and I'm humble too."

Everyone would laugh and, just as planned, the professor would immediately make a note on the class attendance sheet. Later I learned that they didn't write "funny guy" but instead wrote "watch this guy." Nonetheless, while all the other students were trying to present themselves as professional and ideal social work "material," I wanted to let people know that I had a sense of humor and that I didn't take myself too seriously. In the process, I conveyed a confidence that appealed to both my colleagues and my professors. In fact, one of my closest friends in graduate school came up to me the first day because she was "impressed" by the way I handled those introductions. Essentially, I was sharing a bit of my personality rather than just telling about my long and illustrious background. In doing so, I created a different type of connection.

Not Another Autograph

My friend and fellow speaker Phil Van Hooser uses a unique tactic when he meets celebrities. Since he travels quite a bit, he often runs into famous people in airports, hotels, and restaurants. Rather than throwing himself at them like a typical fan asking for an autograph, he approaches the celebrity by saying, "Excuse me _____ [he'll call them by name], I couldn't help but recognize you. I am familiar with your work [he'll give examples]. In my work, I help people enhance their leadership skills. As a recognized leader in your field, do you mind sharing your perspectives on what makes a person an effective leader?"

Unlike most fans, Phil does not approach celebrities by saying, "I'm your biggest fan," or, "I'm a singer too!" Instead, he knows that he has a greater chance of connecting by getting them to talk about what they know and love. Most times, they respond positively, and sometimes they'll have a lengthy conversation with him.

And this is another key to making successful connections with others.

Focus on the other person.

I realize this is diametrically opposed to the title of this chapter, but it's the heart of human connections. People generally prefer talking about themselves to joining *us* in a conversation about *us*. So, if we'll let them do that, they'll remember us as a great listener who was interested in *them*.

But why is connecting with others important? That's how we develop relationships that keep us from being disconnected from the world. I believe that it is the essential ingredient in our human-to-human contact. Making a personal connection allows us to create community, even though our community may include people from other jobs, cities, and cultures. Additionally, these human connections allow us to know more than we currently know because they expand our knowledge through the knowledge of others.

When I buy a new car, I'll ask friends what models they like. When I switched from a PC to a Mac, I contacted two colleagues and asked them about their experience with the same transition. These connections not only enriched my life but made the changes in my life easier. Another key outcome of good connections is business development. Most business owners know that there is a greater likelihood of new business by connecting, in a positive way, with more people.

In his book *The Tipping Point*, Malcolm Gladwell describes the different types of people who tend to spread ideas through their interactions with others. One is actually called the Connector. Connectors are networkers who have a lot of people connections. They seem to know something about everything and they know people who can help anyone. When we need information or another human resource, these Connectors connect us to someone who can help. It could be a doctor, a lawyer, or a mole infestation specialist (the yard kind, not the skin kind). To me, they are the best kind of networker because they have what seems to be an endless supply of resources.

If we approached every social or professional situation with the goal of connecting to people and connecting people to things they need, we would begin to expand our sphere of influence tremendously. Others would begin connecting us to the things we need. And once again, it's because we are focused on others and not ourselves. Yet, in the end, we also get what we need. It's like being narcissistic in an altruistic way.

The Well-Fun-Connecting Process

I heard a story of a woman who was attending a national conference for the large company in which she worked. During one of the breaks, she was sitting at a table having coffee when a man sat down beside her. She smiled and after a few seconds, she leaned over to the man and said, "This is the most boring conference I've ever attended. I think I'm going to skip the keynote speech and go to the beach for the afternoon."

The man looked at her and said, "Do you know who I am?"
She said, "No."

He said, "I'm one of the senior vice presidents and I'm giving the keynote speech this afternoon."

She said, "Do you know who I am?"

He said, "No."

So she got up and left.

OK, so this is not the best way to network even though it's a great way to get out of a difficult situation. And yet, you'd be surprised at how many people try to connect with others by assuming they have something in common without really getting to know the other person first.

The following are some tips on how to make the most of our connecting opportunities. And let's be clear. Every time we are with another human being, it's a connection opportunity. And if we keep this simple principle in mind, we'll become the king or queen of connectors. It's not about us. With that in mind, try these:

Do It Well

1. The way that we are remembered, and the way we remember others, is through something we have in common. When we first start talking with another person, **we should try to find something in common**. Perhaps it's our place of birth, our educational background, our hobby, or our love of Heather Locklear. Whatever it is, we should see if we can find it early in the conversation.

2. One of the best ways to make someone else feel valued and important is to **ask them questions**. Don't immediately go for the big ticket items such as their view on abortion or whether they voted Democrat or Republican. Instead, ask about their work, their family, and their hobbies. The more you learn about them, the better you'll be able to connect to and with them.

3. **Determine if there is any way you can help** the other person. It's a little awkward to say, "How can I help you?" But in the midst of the conversation, if you're listening, you'll see needs they might have. Then you can try to connect them with resources they need whenever possible.

Make It Fun

1. We know from numerous research studies that **people are attracted to people with a sense of humor**. If we develop our humor aptitude, we will attract more people because we all love to laugh. A bit of appropriate humor (i.e., not offensive or off-color) will make us much more appealing and approachable.

2. **Find a funny way to describe what you do** so that when people ask, you're not giving the stereotypical elevator speech. When I used to speak on injecting humor into healthcare, I often told people that I was in the business of making colonoscopies more fun. It always elicited a laugh and then a follow-up question or two.

3. When you meet someone new, **ask them the funniest thing that has happened** in their line of work or in the last 48 hours. It's a great conversation starter and it keeps you from getting bored right from the start.

Making an effort to get to know others and help them get their needs met is the most effective way to keep human contact alive. George Bailey did this in *It's a Wonderful Life*. And even when he felt he was at the end of his rope, he was described as the "richest man in town."

Chapter 14

All for Fun and Fun for All

Most of us enter the professional world understanding that we must work with other people but not really understanding that means working *with* other people. I was lucky to begin my career in hospice care, because our services were delivered through an interdisciplinary team of professionals. Most working teams are actually multidisciplinary. In other words, they are groups of professionals who work together, but each professional focuses on his/her area of expertise independent of the others. An interdisciplinary team, on the other hand, integrates the work of each team member as a way to enhance the services to the customers, or in the case of hospice, the patients.

Our hospice team included a nurse, a doctor, a social worker, a chaplain, and other professionals as needed. We met weekly, and when we worked with a patient or family, we consulted each other as a way to improve each of our individual services. If a patient was not interested in seeing the chaplain, the nurse and social worker would consult with the chaplain to learn how to meet any spiritual needs that might come up. We weren't giving communion or performing exorcisms, but we did learn how to use our colleagues' expertise within our own work.

The problem with most organizations is that there is inherent competition between team members. Often we're vying for the same bonuses, the same promotions, or even that same bag of Cool Ranch Doritos that someone left on the counter in the break room. This can get competitive and antagonistic. So while we talk a good game about being a team player, we're often just trying to outshine our colleagues.

Banding Together

In college, I was part of the University of Virginia Pep Band. We were the highlight of the football games back in the 1970s and 1980s because the football team was terrible. However, today, the Pep Band no longer performs because, once the football team improved, the university wanted a "real" band. Prior to that, our band was a funny, satirical band that told jokes during halftime instead of performing the usual regimented (see "boring") marching shows.

For instance, when we played our arch rivals, Virginia Tech, the announcer would say something like this: "I'm sorry to interrupt the halftime performance, but we have a news bulletin to report. Last night, Virginia Tech's library burned down . . . and both books were lost…and unfortunately, one wasn't even colored in yet."

The band would then form the shape of a library on the field and play *Disco Inferno*. I know, very clever.

The halftime shows were so funny, many people came to the game just to see the band. As one of the Pep Band writers once said, "The biggest challenge for the band was writing something funnier than the first half of football."

Now that's funny.

Not surprisingly, whenever an opponent came to our stadium, we made fun of them. However, whenever we traveled to an opponent's stadium, we made fun of their traditional rival. We knew that if we made fun of *their* rivals in their stadium, we would succeed in winning *them* over. That's how teams work. They work together, not against each other. We weren't idiots. We weren't going to set ourselves up for failure.

For instance, when we played Georgia Tech, we made a joke about the girls at the University of Georgia. The Georgia Tech fans loved it. They loved it so much, in fact, when their own band started performing, the fans started chanting, "Bring back Virginia." It doesn't get any better than that.

From a team perspective, you could say that we were joining together with our opponents, as a team against *their* rivals.

The Obligatory Sports Analogy

As of 2011, the overall assist leader of the NBA is John Stockton, the former point guard for the Utah Jazz. Over the course of his career, he made 15,806 assists, meaning that he passed the ball nearly 16,000 times to someone else who scored. He also holds the record for steals, for most games played, for most seasons played, and for most consecutive games played. However, John Stockton is not even in the top 25 for total points scored—which is the stat that most players and fans cherish.

To me, John Stockton is the essence of teamwork. He holds five major records in the NBA, but most of us don't think of him as a superstar. Instead, we think of Michael Jordan, Kareem Abdul-Jabbar, and Kobe Bryant. Stockton, however, consistently showed up more than any other player. He created more opportunities for others to score than any other player. And he stole the ball more than any other player. He worked hard to *assist* the team rather than *stealing* the spotlight for himself.

How often do you see that in your own work environment?

A Brush With Celebrity

Early in my career, I had the privilege of being invited to emcee an event with actor Tony Randall. Tony had been successful on stage, screen, and television. Most memorably, he played Felix Unger on the television show *The Odd Couple*. When I was invited to emcee with him, I was asked to write schtick for him to perform as part of our emcee "routine." Now, let me put this in the proper and awkward perspective. Tony Randall had been a comedic actor for nearly 50 years. I was a young humorist with a few years of experience writing funny halftime shows at college football games. There was no way I was qualified to write comedy for Felix Unger. To make matters worse, Tony, a 76-year-old widower, had recently married a 26-year-old woman. The coordinator for the event also wanted me to make fun of his young wife. All I could think of was how I was about to destroy my career before it even got started.

I was given Tony Randall's home phone number and told to talk with him about our "routine." I called him and filled him in on all the details. I told him that I did *not* feel comfortable writing for him. He agreed, and he told me to perform my own material and then he'd simply ad-lib. He was very good at this and some of his funniest appearances on the *Tonight Show* were due to his witty ad-libbing.

Just before the call ended, I mustered up the courage to ask him about poking fun at his marriage. He laughed and invited me to say anything I wanted about the situation. He said, "The press has had a field day with it, so you should too."

I was relieved after the conversation but then developed a new anxiety. I would be performing, for the first time in my life, with a huge star. How could someone like me be funny or even noticeable next to him? What had I gotten myself into?

A few days before the event, I developed the worst case of bronchitis I've ever had (no coincidence I'm sure). My doctor loaded me up with medications to get me through the event. I got there early, swallowed a bunch of pills, and went down the pre-event gathering to meet Tony and check the room. He was delightfully social and very generous with his time and conversation.

After dinner, we were introduced and the two of us took the stage. I opened our routine by saying how much I appreciated the opportunity to work with him. I then turned to him and said, "Tony, even though we come from very different backgrounds, we have more in common than you may realize."

He said, "Is that right?"

I said, "Yes. For one, we both married 26-year-olds. [Comedy pause.] I was just 27 when *I* did it!"

He laughed. The crowd laughed. And the rest of the evening was a great success.

But the key to the routine was working out our roles together before we went onstage. Even though we eventually did our own separate routines, we had worked out the expectation, as if we were a team, beforehand, and we didn't view it as a competition for the spotlight.

Building on the Power of Great Teamwork

Back in late 1970s or early 1980s, the Building Industry Association of San Diego organized a competition to break the world record for building a house from scratch. I'm not exactly sure what "scratch" means, but essentially, they had to build a house from bottom to top. In order to have a shot at the record, they needed all of the trades to work closely together to pull it off. They created two teams of 400 workers and challenged them to compete against each other. It made the world record attempt more exciting, and more fun.

Each area of the house was built in separate sections. But the workers had mapped out the pieces beforehand, so they knew each piece would fit together when the house was finished. In the end, the roof, walls, foundation, appliances, and landscaping of the winning house were assembled in two hours and 45 minutes. And the house met all of the local building codes to boot. It was amazing. But it could not have happened unless everyone worked together extremely well. It was the ultimate in cooperation *and* it set a world record.

The Well-Fun-Team Process

Someone once said that if two people exchange a penny, they each still have a penny. However, if they exchange ideas, they now each have two ideas. This concept is at the core of working with others. None of us are experts at everything, so we must tap into the expertise and experiences of others to broaden and enhance our own abilities.

So what does it take to become a good team member?

Do It Well

1. First, **make sure your team knows what the goals of the team are and what the specific roles of each team member are.** The blind leading the blind only works when team members are actually blind. If we don't know what we're supposed to do and who's supposed to do it, how can we work together to get it done?

2. **Run effective team meetings**. Almost every team has meetings. And almost every team meeting is poorly run. To make the team work better, the meetings must run better. There is a chapter in this book on running meetings. So, read it. Enough said?

3. **Nip conflict in the bud**. All teams have conflict. And not all conflict is bad. But unattended conflict can undermine

the work of the team. The most effective teams address conflict when it arises and work together to resolve it. See the chapter in this book on conflict to learn how. Seriously, don't make me come over there.

Make It Fun

1. **Recruit fun people** for teams. You should have several people on your team who will liven up the meetings and the work. A funny and creative member can totally change the dynamic of the team.

2. **Find fun and creative ways to support each other**. Finely tuned teams not only help each other accomplish their goals, but they also make each member feel valued and part of something important. Publicly acknowledge team members, bring candy to meetings, have a meeting over pizza, or give out hundred-dollar bills. OK, that last one is a stretch, but find out what makes the team happy and do it.

3. **Encourage humor and creativity in the work of the team**. Most team leaders are so serious about the end result, they forget to make the process fun for the team. Consider competitions, skits, nicknames, and songs as ways to make normal team processes more interesting and creative.

Teamwork. All for one, one for all, and all for fun.

Chapter 15

Don't Make Me Come Over There

Whenever someone disagrees with me or challenges my integrity, something in the pit of my stomach turns and I feel a burst of adrenaline shoot through my body. It's that instinctual fight-or-flight mechanism preparing me for battle, and it's the same mechanism that saved most of our ancestors from being eaten by wild animals.

If the disagreement or challenge occurs in a dark alley and involves more than a dozen people, my instinct is flight. If the challenge occurs anywhere else, such as a customer service situation or in the workplace, I'm drawn toward the conflict. I'm not sure if it's a need to be right (which I'm often not) or simply the challenge of the battle that excites me. All I know is that I can argue with the best of them.

My first successful conflict was in Mrs. Sturgill's sixth-grade class. Mrs. Sturgill was a large woman with big hair who would sit at her desk behind a big wicker purse, twirling her hair while peering into mirror on her desk. It was very intimidating and just a bit creepy.

Most of us were afraid of Mrs. Sturgill, even though we never saw her eat a child or bury one in the playground.

When we were working on an assignment, she would look out from behind her purse every few minutes to see if we were behaving. If she caught someone, she would assign her favorite punishment—writing proverbs. If a kid got out of his seat or was talking to his neighbor, Mrs. Sturgill would tell him to write "A rolling stone gathers no moss" 500 times or "A bird in the hand is worth two in the bush" 400 times. I supposed it wasn't as bad as being eaten, or buried in the playground, and we did learn a lot of proverbs. A *lot* of proverbs.

One day, Mrs. Sturgill told us to work quietly at our desks. The obvious problem was that, as sixth graders, we didn't yet have the skills to work quietly at our desks. Our sit-quietly-and-focus gland had not fully developed. So, as was our nature, we talked. After reminding us to be quiet roughly 27 times, Mrs. Sturgill came out from behind the wicker purse and slammed her fist down on the desk. She said, "You boys and girls would talk until doomsday if I'd let you."

I raised my hand.

"What?" she said.

"Well, wouldn't that put an end to it? . . . The talking?"

Several kids laughed. Some went pale. Several ducked under their desks in case she reached for the wicker purse.

Mrs. Sturgill covered a snicker. Then, she composed herself and said, "Ronnie Culberson, I want you to write 'Look before you leap' 40 times."

I was shocked. She said 40. The punishment was always 500, or at least 400. No one ever got just 40.

I thought to myself, "I'm onto something here!"

Clearly, I had won the conflict. It was a small victory for sixth graders everywhere and for the power of a little humor in the face of adversity.

I only wish that every conflict was that easy to resolve. Unfortunately, it's not. When we find ourselves in arguments, we often assume a defensive posture, not because we feel strongly about something important but because our egos are frail and we have been challenged. Our feelings of inadequacy surface and we need to prove our worth. Or we hear the voice of an abusive father in the comments of our opponent and we react to that father instead of the reality of the situation. Then the conflict gets blown way out of proportion and we find ourselves reacting as if our life hangs in the balance. And most times, it does not.

The key to managing conflict is to first and foremost recognize that we are different from other people—even though we have similarities. We each have our own values, priorities, and perspectives. Then, when we come into close proximity with others who have different values, priorities, and perspectives, we attempt to turn them into us as if their being like us would be better. In reality, having lots of usses would be rather boring.

If everyone preferred vanilla ice cream, we would never get to experience the hot chili and basil ice cream I had in a funky restaurant last year. If everyone drove Fords, we would never experience the Lexus. And if everyone preferred conservative clothing, we'd never enjoy the understated attire at Hooters. See, differences are good.

What Would Jesus Do . . . to Moses?

Look at the divisions that religion has created. We've got Christianity, Judaism, Islam, Hinduism, and many others. Within each religion, there have also been many splits because the participants can't agree on their beliefs.

One of my favorite religious jokes is about a man who was rescued from a small deserted island. When the rescuers came ashore, they saw three separate buildings. They asked the man what the buildings were for.

He said, "Well, that first one is my house. The second one is my church. And the third one is where I used to go to church."

It's sad but true. Because we can't resolve conflicts about beliefs we hold dear, we create new organizations with people who think like we do. That is, until they no longer think like we do and then we leave them, looking for others who do think like we do—at least for the time being.

The same differences occur in politics as well. There is as much fighting about the fact that we don't agree as there is about the issues being debated. It's an either-or mentality, and until we're able to see other options, we will continue to have unresolved conflict.

DeWitt Jones, a former *National Geographic* photographer and now a powerful motivational speaker, teaches people about the "other right answer." Through stories using his powerful photographs, he explains how he would capture a photograph one way and then change his perspective in order to find an even better photograph from another angle. If he had stayed locked into one way of viewing the particular scene, he would never have seen all of the possibilities. His is a great lesson for us.

A Kinder, Gentler, and Funnier Conflict

A older gentleman was having trouble with a group of kids who kept throwing rocks in his yard. When he told them to stop, they ignored them. So, one day, he told them he would give them a dollar for each day they threw rocks in his yard. A week later, he told them he would give them fifty cents for each day they threw rocks at his trees. The third week, he told them he would give them a dime for each day they threw rocks.

At this point, one of the kids looked at him and said, "Nah, it ain't worth it."

It was a very funny and creative solution that most of us would never consider when we're in the midst of a heated conflict with someone else. And that may be one of our biggest barriers to resolving conflict. It feels too emotional, and sometimes our emotions react before our brains do.

Humor is a great tool to manage conflict (and our brains) and to take the personal nature out of it.

The Well-Fun-Conflict Process

So, how do we handle conflict well? It's really quite simple but it requires that we not be married to our own views to the point that we can't see another's perspective. Here are my suggestions:

Do It Well

1. **Identify the source of the conflict.** Is it a difference in values, information, goals, or methods? Once we identify the source, we can explore the differences. A difference in information is easy to resolve. A difference in values is more difficult and more personal.

2. **Discuss (not argue) the vested interests** of each person in the source of the conflict. Why is the issue important? What does each of you gain or lose if a decision is made?

3. **Brainstorm all creative options for compromise.** Choose the best possible win-win solution. Instead of looking at the conflict as a potential lose-lose, consider it a win-win. And remember, often winning is simply getting some portion of what you want rather than everything you want.

Make It Fun

1. **Use humor to avoid conflict in the first place.** When you find yourself going down the path of self-defensiveness or protecting your ego, you can turn the tables and use a bit of self-deprecating humor. You may avoid the conflict altogether. If you can laugh at yourself, you're less likely to become inflamed by someone else.

2. When you find yourself becoming heated about a conflict, you need to **take a humor break.** Get out of the situation,

if possible, and distract the mind by watching a funny video or reading something humorous. The break will give you time to regain your perspective. Then, if you're still heated, the other person is probably wrong and you can hit them in the nose (just kidding).

3. As you brainstorm possible options, you should **use humor and fun during the brainstorming process** to take the heaviness of the conflict out of the equation. Try a creative competition for finding a out-of-the box solution or DeWitt's "other right answer."

Conflict is inevitable. But that doesn't mean we can't find value in our differences. Argue well, but make it fun.

Section 3:

All Work and No Play Is, Well, Work

Chapter 16

Take My Job . . . Please

When it comes to work, we should either do what we love or do something else.

The core work-related benefit of Do It Well, Make It Fun is that by combining excellence and fun, we will design our career path so that we succeed *and* enjoy each point along the way. To be perfectly honest, I didn't *love* every job I had, but when any job stopped being fun, I started looking for something else. However, no matter what the job was, I did the best possible job I could and tried to make the experience of my work enjoyable.

As I described earlier, I had my sights on medical school. Unfortunately, I didn't have my sights on the grades required to get into medical school. I wasn't a bad student. In fact, I was above average at an above-average school. But I was also in the band. And I was also in a fraternity. And I was also in love with my future wife. So, my focus was spread somewhat evenly between all my pursuits, which meant that my grades got about one-fourth of my focus.

My professors, however, were more narrow-minded than I was

and, outrageously, they believed that I should have spent most of my time in college focusing on my grades. But my medical school advisor was different. He told me, "We have different priorities at different points in our lives. Studying was not your priority, which is fine. But now, if you really want to get into medical school, you need to make grades your priority. Go to graduate school and get all A's. Then, you can apply to medical school and you'll probably get in."

So, I went to work in the psychiatric unit of the University of Virginia Medical Center where, I should point out, there was always a fine line between patients and staff, and applied to graduate school in social work. I was accepted, I loved it, and I got straight A's. But by then, I wanted be a social worker instead of a doctor—especially after living with two medical students and watching as medical school took two perfectly normal men and turned them into two sleep-deprived, cranky, and overly educated physicians. It's no wonder that bedside manner can get lost in the bureaucracy of the medical hierarchy.

Meanwhile, I felt fulfilled with my grad school experience and began the search for a social work job. A huge influence on me, at that point in my life, was my nephew Allen's death. I was quite taken with the fact that, at 25 years of age, I had not experienced a really close death. Coincidentally, within a year, two childhood girlfriends died in car accidents. Both deaths were difficult to comprehend. But because of these experiences, I was led to a career in hospice. I was hired as a home care social worker at Hospice of Northern Virginia, and it would be one of the best experiences of my life.

When I first met with my supervisor, I was warned that the staff sometimes engaged in gallows humor as a way to deal with stress. My boss told me not to be offended by it, because it was their way of coping. I thought, "This is right up my alley."

And speaking of alley, there was an alley behind the hospice building with a sign that said, "Dead End."

Now that's funny. But I digress.

The hospice staff was wonderful, and I have never worked any-where where the employees were as committed to the work and appreciated the joys in life as they did. And it made sense. Every day, they witnessed death, so humor and fun were welcome allies.

But two and half years into the job, the stress of the organization took its toll. The work was rewarding but the senior management was not providing good leadership. I didn't agree with decisions that were made, nor did I like the way staff was treated. I left for greener pastures, so I thought, working in the Division of Child Protection at Children's National Medical Center in Washington, DC. In other words, I went from hospice care to child abuse. Is it possible to have any more fun than that?

A New Direction

Children's was a wonderful hospital where I discovered that working with kids was quite different from working with adults. Kids tend to be much more resilient. A seven-year-old could be bandaged from head to foot with life-threatening injuries and he would still want to play. An adult took to the bed for weeks because of an infected hangnail.

Unfortunately, my office at Children's was in Southeast DC, one of the most dangerous parts of the city. As a country boy who grew up in a town of 280 people, this was a tough transition for me. The culture of the inner city troubled me. The poverty, the drugs, and the fact that I was an outsider made it a harder environment than working in the more familiar suburbs. My colleagues were great, though. We had long conversations about race, the city life, and our different experiences growing up. I marveled at their commitment to child protection and I longed to be as committed as they were. Child advocates are a special breed of people. They sacrifice so much to make sure children are safe. I didn't have the same drive. I cared, but the passion wasn't there. So, after six months, I knew I had to move on or else my work would suffer.

Soon after my decision to leave Children's, I noticed that my old boss's position at Hospice of Northern Virginia had opened up.

The CEO had also resigned, so there was new leadership. It was an opportunity to get back to the work I loved. I applied for the job and, surprisingly, at the age of 29 years, I became a manager. It was the hardest and yet the most rewarding job I ever had.

In my four years as counseling manager, I went from supervising six people to supervising 26 people. There were so many staff members, I had to outsource some of the licensed supervision the social workers needed since I couldn't do it all myself. But this was a time when my Do It Well, Make It Fun philosophy shone. I read everything I could get my hands on and, to be bluntly honest and with very little humility, I became a pretty darn good manager.

But we also had a lot of fun. We had funny rituals to welcome new staff. We held an annual celebration evening for our staff and volunteers during which I dressed in drag as a way to shake things up a bit. We even had elaborate going-away parties for employees who had been with us for a while.

In my fourth year as counseling manager, my job was eliminated. The CEO felt that we no longer needed a full-time counseling manager but that we could use a director of quality service. They offered me the job. The decision devastated my staff, but in the name of efficiency, I had actually worked myself out of the job by creating some very effective support systems. And, honestly, I was ready for a new opportunity. I just regret that my staff paid the price of losing a manager and an ally.

As director of quality service, I got the best training I've ever had. I spent four days at the Institute for Healthcare Improvement and learned everything about quality improvement. I took that knowledge and started the first quality improvement and customer service program for my hospice. I did over a hundred training programs in all aspects of quality and customer service. Many of the things I learned then I'm still using today. And the best part was, I honed my speaking *and* my humor skills. The experience has translated to my being a much better speaker today.

At the same time, I was speaking at national conferences and was getting a number of requests to speak for other organizations. As the requests increased, I realized that my true calling was in professional speaking. So I left hospice in 1996 to become a speaker, author, and humorist.

I miss the hospice work. I also miss the hospice staff. And I truly miss the patients and families. But I'm using everything I learned in that job to reach people in a new way today.

Take This Job and LUV It

I realize that this rambling story may not teach you much, but I hope the tone has come through loud and clear. Many people spend 40, 50, or even 60 hours a week in a job. If we are spending that much time in anything, it needs to be rewarding, fulfilling, and fun. If we don't love it, I'm totally convinced there is either something else out there for us *or* we just need to figure out how to make our current job more fun.

Nobody gets to the end of their life and wishes they had done more of the boring, mundane, and laborious aspects of their work. Instead, as my experience in hospice showed, they wished they had gone on more vacations. They wished they had spent more time with loved ones. They wished they had spent 15 minutes to save 15% or more on their car insurance. They never wish they had earned more overtime. Because Southwest Airlines is full of people who embrace this perspective, I decided to check them out and see what really goes on in this unique corporate culture.

The name plate on the receptionist's desk said, "Director of First Impressions" (DFI). An airplane oxygen mask hung from the ceiling over her seat while a bobble-head doll of the CEO nodded at me from the counter surrounding her desk. Debbie, the Director of First Impressions, leapt from behind the counter, hugged me, and said, "You must be Ron, the FUN guy. We've been waiting to meet you.

And by the way, this is Southwest Airlines—we don't do handshakes here!"

I was speechless (no easy task). This was not the typical stuffy corporate office. This was the People Department of Southwest Airlines and I was important enough to be greeted by name and with a hug.

Mary McMurtry, the regional manager for Field Employment at Southwest's Baltimore office, had graciously agreed to show me around their office and talk to me about the culture of Southwest. For a humor professional, this was like finding the Holy Grail, meeting Bob Hope, or receiving a gold-plated whoopee cushion. Southwest Airlines has not only held a place in the top five best places to work in the United States, it is one of the most FUN companies in the country.

The airline began service in 1971 and has more than 34,000 employees managing 2,800 flights a day. They carried over 65 million passengers in 2003 through 58 cities in 30 states. One year they received over 200,000 resumes for 908 new employee positions. Southwest was ranked by the Department of Transportation as the airline having the fewest complaints for thirteen consecutive years and was rated the most admired airline for 7+ years in *Fortune* magazine.

But back to my visit. After Debbie informed Mary that I was in a "holding pattern," Mary quickly appeared in the lobby to greet me. Hug number two. Then, she escorted me into her office, which was decorated with dozens of Wizard of Oz photos, a framed copy of Southwest's anniversary poster, another bobble-head doll of former CEO Herb Kelleher, and a fluffy red boa strung around her desk. At any minute, I expected dancing flight attendants to take my drink order!

Over the course of the next two hours, Mary shared with me the unusual and amazingly relaxed atmosphere of employment at Southwest Airlines. I began to understand that "relaxed" does not refer to an attitude of indifference or apathy but instead refers to a way of operating that supports results, customers, and staff over restrictive policies and procedures. One of the most important groups responsible for maintaining that attitude is the Culture Committee, a group of employees who are responsible for making sure the culture and the FUN stay intact.

The Culture Committee organizes fund-raisers to pay for monthly parties and celebrations throughout the year. For instance, they might sell Mother's Day flowers to employees for a nominal fee and use the proceeds to pay for a Monday Night Football party or Cinco de Mayo celebration. The biggest fund-raiser is a golf tournament that supports Ronald McDonald House Charities, Southwest's corporate charity. The airline has contributed more than $6 million to this charity over an 18-year period.

My favorite experience at Southwest was hearing about the practical jokes that are played on new and seasoned employees. Delta (an interesting name for someone working at Southwest, don't you think?), a new hire, had to complete and return a multiple-page application form to the People Department prior to her start date. When she stopped by one day to drop off the forms, the lobby was full of job candidates waiting for interviews. The minute she came into the lobby, all of the candidates stood up and sang all of the verses to the song "Delta Dawn." The office broke out in hysterics!

Another time, a senior executive spent a day working at the ticket counter and with the ground crew to have a better understanding of their roles. While she was helping direct a plane to the gate using those long, orange directional devices, one of the seasoned ground crew members told her to rotate her wrists in a circular manner. When she did this, the plane did a 360-degree turn! She began to scream, thinking she had sent a confusing signal to the pilot. In reality, the ground crew had contacted the pilot and told him they had a "greeny" directing the plane and that they wanted to have some fun with her. The pilot enthusiastically agreed to play along.

I recall that Herb Kelleher once said, "If work was more fun, it would feel less like work." In a nutshell, that's what it's like to work for Southwest Airlines. It's about working hard and serving others. It's about hugs and humor for the new kid on the block. It's about creating a culture that means something. It's all about focusing on the most important asset they have—their people. I guess that's why their company logo says "LUV."

The Well-Fun-Work Process

Here are tips for making your work more productive and more enjoyable:

Do It Well

1. **Know the difference between a job and a career**. Often we take a job to pay the bills. But it's just a job. A career, on the other hand, aligns with your passion, your gifts, and your skills and is that thing to which you feel called. It's fine to take a job as long as you keep your sights on a career.

2. **Never accept that you are stuck** in any job or a career and that you have no other choices. There is always something out there that's better than what you currently have. It may not be easy to find and it may not be right in front of you. But it's there. Be patient and open to ideas, and look for opportunities.

3. Once in the job, **determine what skills you perform well and what skills you need to improve**. You can't just show up. Instead, you show up and do a good job. That might require that you attend a class, read an excellent book (like this one), or get an advanced degree to develop your skills. You'll be amazed at how much fun work can be when you get better at it.

Make It Fun

1. Every single day, when you arrive at work, **ask yourself how you are going to make the day more fun**. It's an attitude thing. If we get to work expecting it to be drudgery, chances are it will be. But if we are open to the possibility that we can actually have fun at work, our chances of going home less stressed improve dramatically.

2. Specifically, **look at every task in your job and see if there is a way to make it more fun**. A funny line in an e-mail makes it more enjoyable to read. A fun activity in a meeting makes it more tolerable to the attendees. Changing your nameplate to "All Knowing Master of Time, Space, and Dimension" is funny (with credit to Steve Martin).

3. **Align yourself with the fun people**. We can't hang out with the "downers." We need to spend time with the people who have a zest for life and who will help keep our work perspective balanced. In meetings, I always sat in the "cut-up corner" with the other fun people. It makes for a much more enjoyable experience.

Work doesn't have to be miserable. Neither do we. With a little thought and effort, we can make work more FUNctional.

Chapter 17

To Do Do Do, Ta Done Done Done

A colleague once suggested that if, each day, I wrote down five things for which I was grateful, my outlook in life would change. And my outlook did change. I became resentful of having to come up with five new gratitudes every single day.

A business mentor suggested that if I accomplished three high-value daily goals, my business would grow, and fame and fortune would follow. I did just what he said for nearly 48 hours. After that, I couldn't seem to maintain the discipline. And coincidentally, growth, fame, and fortune did not follow me anywhere.

I've had a lifelong love-hate relationship with to-do lists. My OCD side loves the organization of a nicely prepared to-do list. And with a memory that's shorter than scientific instruments can measure, I need a lot of help remembering all I need to do. A few years ago, I was sitting in my office and realized that I was supposed to be at a meeting with a prospective client. I immediately called the client and apologized for my idiotic blunder. She was very gracious, and we rescheduled the meeting. I sent a gift as an attempt to temper my guilt, but in the end, I think the client was unimpressed with my lack of organization.

But it could have been worse. A speaker friend of mine was sitting in his office one afternoon when his phone rang. His client said, "You are supposed to be here delivering a keynote address—right now." He checked his calendar and sure enough, he was supposed to be at a conference two hours away. There was no way he could get there, and the client was more than a bit miffed. I can so relate. I've never missed a speaking engagement because I forgot, but it's the kind of thing that keeps me up at night.

Even though my OCD causes me to be organized, my organization structures get a bit complicated and I tend to be a bit less functional than I'd like to be. So, over the years, I've tried several thousand systems for creating to-do lists that actually work. The key for me is prioritizing effectively and then staying focused on getting the priorities completed.

If you have ever read *The 7 Habits of Highly Effective People* by Stephen Covey, you may remember a grid from the book that separates everything we have to do into four categories. Below is that grid:

Important & Urgent	Important & Not Urgent
Not Important & Urgent	Not Important & Not Urgent

Covey urges us to focus on Important and Not Urgent items because these items usually deal with long-term strategy and planning and will give us greater results. All of the other boxes force us to deal with items that, in the big scheme of things, don't really move us toward our goals—things like e-mail, telemarketing calls, meetings, and dusting the inside of our file cabinet (unless of course the file cabinet is so dusty it won't open).

When it comes to managing to-do lists well, we need to know our priorities and then organize them in a way that makes us more effective. After that, we need to find a way to make the to-do process more fun.

Task Masters

I wrote the bulk of this book while holed up in our beach house in Duck, NC. As inspiration, I read Stephen King's book *On Writing*. It's a wonderful book about the craft of writing, and it's interwoven with a memoir of King's life. When he talks about the discipline it requires to pursue a writing career, he suggests writing 2,000 words per day, or roughly ten typed pages. I read that and realized that I've never come anywhere close to writing 2,000 words per day and yet I consider myself a writer. While I was in Duck, I averaged about 7,000 words per day, but that's because I committed to this process for 5 days and focused all my work time on it. But if we apply Stephen King's suggestion to Stephen Covey's grid and remember Malcolm Gladwell's 10,000 hours, the reason we don't get any better and the reason we don't get the big stuff done is that we focus too much on the urgent and unimportant tasks.

My heroes are those people like Stephen King who are so focused that they won't even entertain interruptions. Andy Stanley is the pastor at North Point Community Church, a large church with several locations in the Atlanta area. Andy did a sermon on workplace issues and described his philosophy of leadership. He said that he believes good leaders know what they do really well and that they must focus on doing those things rather than trying to improve the things they don't do well. One of the things he does well is preach. He knows that his sermons are a big reason that people come to North Point. So, when a member of the congregation wants to take him to lunch, he'll respond, "The very thing you like about this church is why I won't go to lunch with you."

If he didn't spend that time working on his sermons, people wouldn't like the church as much. He has cracked the code for excellence and he's doing things well by staying focused.

I don't know if I'm a great speaker but I *am* a very good one. I am a decent writer. I'm not a Stephen King or an Anne Lamott, but a decent writer. Both are my gifts, but I could be a whole lot better. The barrier keeping me from getting better is that I'm spending too much time on my urgent and unimportant tasks each day and not enough time on the important but not urgent items. If my sweet spot is speaking and writing, then I need to spend the majority of my day writing and speaking (or working on my speaking when I'm not actually speaking).

So, a well-done to-do list is laser focused and geared toward long-term success.

My mother-in-law sent me this list of Thomas Jefferson's accomplishments. It's humbling to see how much he accomplished, but I'm sure it was because he was focused (and didn't have e-mail!).

- At 5, began studying under his cousin's tutor.

- At 9, studied Latin, Greek, and French.

- At 14, studied classical literature and additional languages.

- At 16, entered the College of William and Mary.

- At 19, studied law for 5 years, starting under George Wythe.

- At 23, started his own law practice.

- At 25, was elected to the Virginia House of Burgesses.

- At 31, wrote the widely circulated "Summary View of the Rights of British America" and retired from his law practice.

- At 32, was a delegate to the Second Continental Congress.

- At 33, wrote the Declaration of Independence.

- At 33, took three years to revise Virginia's legal code and wrote a public education bill and a statute for religious freedom.

- At 36, was elected the second governor of Virginia, succeeding Patrick Henry.

- At 40, served in Congress for two years.

- At 41, was the American minister to France and negotiated commercial treaties with European nations along with Ben Franklin and John Adams.

- At 46, served as the first secretary of state under, George Washington.

- At 53, served as vice president and was elected president of the American Philosophical Society.

- At 55, drafted the Kentucky Resolutions and became the active head of Republican Party.

- At 57, was elected the third president of the United States.

- At 60, obtained the Louisiana Purchase, doubling the nation's size.

- At 61, was elected to a second term as president.

- At 80, helped President Monroe shape the Monroe Doctrine.

- At 81, almost single-handedly created the University of Virginia and served as its first president.

I'm a bit tired just writing what he did. I can't imagine what his to-do list looked like, but I suspect he always had his eye on the big-ticket items.

The Well-Fun-To-Done Process

To keep our to-do lists manageable while focusing on the right things, we must pay attention to the following:

Do It Well

1. **Identify your sweet spots,** the big-ticket items that will lead you down the path of reaching your goals by tapping into your gifts, skills, and passions. These are the long-term targets that lead to you ultimate success in life and work.

2. **Create a list of goals that must get done this week.** What MUST get done this week to keep you in line with the sweet spots? If you're writing a book with 25 chapters and you want to get it done in one year, that's roughly a chapter every two weeks. So your weekly goal would be to write a chapter one week and edit it the next.

3. **Create a list of the three most important things that must get done today** to meet the goals for the week and keep focused on the sweet spots. Now you take your weekly goals and break them into 5 days (or the number of days you have available). Don't do anything else until each of these goals is completed.

Make It Fun

1. **Find ways to make working on the sweet spot items fun.** I went to our beach house alone to write. Sometimes I go to Starbucks where I can enjoy music, the hustle and bustle of people, and my favorite latte. Sometimes, I just crank loud music to entertain me while I work on a project that does not require too much concentration. We can do whatever turns us on. Just make it fun.

2. Consider **developing a few fun to-do list items that you can tackle after you're finished with the high-value items.** Watch an episode of your favorite show on Hulu or treat yourself to an ice cream cone. Dangle a fun carrot in front of your work to make the accomplishment a little more worthwhile.

3. **Keep a tote board of progress** on the goals, just like the telethons on TV do. When you get to the end of the year, you'll be amazed by what you've done—that is, if you've kept your focus.

To-Do It Well and To-Do It Fun will lead To Success.

Chapter 18

In Other Words

Several years into my career, I had established myself as a humorist. I was speaking all over the country on the practical value of humor. My programs were very funny, but there was also take-home value that my audience members could apply directly to their life and work. At the time, I was a member of a mastermind group. Our group was comprised of six speakers who met monthly to help each other with business goals, presentation ideas, and other areas of our work. It was a great way to escape the solitary life of speaking and writing and to get objective input from peers who knew what we were going through. I've been involved in a number of mastermind groups over the years and each has been a great experience.

During one of those groups, my friend and colleague Bill Cates looked at my promotional brochure and said, "This isn't funny."

He was exposing the fact that I promote myself as a humorist, and yet my marketing materials were not funny.

Bill said, "Don't you think a humorist's material should be funny?"

He made a great point and I immediately re-crafted the marketing copy and added statements such as "I love this guy" as a testimonial from my wife and that I was "cheaper than big-name celebrities" and that "no animals were harmed in my presentations."

It made a huge difference in how I was perceived, and it reinforced my message that humor is an effective communication tool.

This concept can also work for other types of communications such as e-mail and voicemail.

Make Your Message Memorable

When I worked at hospice, we had just gotten an internal e-mail that eventually replaced the inter-office memo. I always made a point to add a funny quote or joke to every e-mail I sent. This doesn't seem so odd today, especially if we've been on the receiving end of the many funny emails that get forwarded to us from everyone we know. That's not what I'm talking about. Instead, I'm talking about making the e-mail message more memorable with a touch of humor. Remember, though, the content of the e-mail had to be good first, before I added the humor.

These days it's easy to become prisoners of e-mail and voicemail. The dings and beeps distract us from the nonurgent but important work. So, we must take control of these valuable technological tools so that we control them rather than letting them control us. In his book *The 4-Hour Workweek* Tim Ferriss explains how to get out from under the control of e-mail and voicemail. For starters, he only checks his e-mail at noon and at the end of the day. He created an auto responder that says that he will respond at those times. That way, no one thinks he's ignoring them. Second, he only checks his voicemail twice a day. This way, he can control the technology rather than being controlled by it.

Handling our e-mail and voicemail involves both the content of the messages and the efficiency in which we reply. If we begin responding to e-mail threads early in the morning, we can spend our entire day in a drawn-out conversation that never seems to end.

Mirthful Messages Are More Memorable

Similar to my problem with dull promotional materials, I had the same issue with my e-mail to prospective clients. Often, it was boring, with only the necessary facts such as "Yes I am available on _____" and "My fee is _____." I decided to change that. Now, when someone contacts me and wants to know my availability and my fee, this is the response they get:

> Thank you for your inquiry. Where did you hear about me?
>
> My speaking fee is _____ plus travel expenses.
>
> Also I require green M&Ms in my dressing room and 20 bottles of lava-filtered water. If you do not have a masseuse onsite, one of your staff will have to rub my shoulders before I go on stage. After my presentation, I will not mingle with the common folk but will sign books as long as everyone stands at least 20 feet away and doesn't look at me. How's that sound?
>
> Seriously, I would love to work with you. I look forward to hearing back from you.

This e-mail has gotten tremendous responses from my prospective clients. One person even said, "We can't afford you this year but I'm going to try my hardest to get you here next year because you sound so fun."

One client took it one step further.

Ethica Health and Retirement Communities is a great organization that manages retirement and long-term care facilities. They asked me to speak at their annual awards program being held at the Ritz Carlton Lodge at Reynolds Plantation outside of Atlanta. I arrived on a cold December day, and when I checked into my room, there was a box of green M&Ms, a personal back massager, and four large bottles of "lava-filtered" water. The labels on the water read, "Lava-Filtered Water from the Volcanoes of North Atlanta."

This client had gone to great lengths to have fun with me after I had had fun with them. Rest assured, if I ever need a real job, the first place I'll apply is Ethica.

Similarly, I always try to create funny messages for my voicemail. I believe that people are tired of hearing "I'm so glad you called and I DO want to talk to you. Please listen for the beep and when you hear it, leave a message. Thank you so much for calling. Make it a super terrific, wonderful, day, week, and weekend."

Ugh.

So, I set off to create different messages every few months that break the normal trend. My favorite went like this: "Hi, this is Ron Culberson. I'm so excited you called because I've got this great new answering machine. Trouble is, I just can't figure out how to (Beep)"

Now I realize this may sound only slightly amusing—or not amusing at all. But 9 out of 10 of my voicemail messages started with laughter before the caller went on to leave a message. How would it feel if your voicemail messages started with laughter? Do you think it would change your attitude that day? Of course it would. Not only do my callers benefit, but so do I.

The Well-Fun-Message Process

In order to manage your e-mail more effectively, here are a few tips:

Do It Well

Manage your e-mail.

1. **Disable the alert** that signals new e-mail or shut down the program completely until the designated time to check e-mail. Not having the distraction will force you into not managing e-mail all day long.

2. **Set aside a specific time to deal with e-mail** (and voice-mail, for that matter). Focus and manage each message by

either responding, deleting, or filing it away. Do not use the inbox as a storage unit. Set up a logical filing system just as you do with other computer files. This makes old messages much easier to find.

3. **Create e-mail templates** or signatures for any repetitive responses made through e-mail.

Manage your voicemail.

Voicemail is similar, although today, there are far more emails than voicemails. Here are some tips for managing your phone calls and voicemail.

1. Reply to a phone message **with a simple e-mail** rather than getting involved in a long conversation.

2. For calls that might take a lot of time to complete, **be prepared with all the information needed**. And if you're calling someone who might "extend" the call beyond its necessary end time, let them know at the beginning of the call that you have a limited amount of time.

3. If you'd rather leave a message at a person's office than talk to him or her, **call at night or on the weekends**.

Make It fun

1. **Use humor in e-mail messages** to make the reading of the e-mail more enjoyable. Make sure it enhances the content and does not detract from it.

2. **Create a funny outgoing message** on voicemail to engage the callers. There are examples on the Internet or you can write our own. Just make sure they're not too long or else callers will get annoyed.

3. When you leave messages for other people, **you should make them light and fun**. After a long workday, it's nice to get fun messages.

If this was helpful, give me a call and leave me a message!

Chapter 19

Turning Hours into Minutes

As the senior management team, we were in a meeting with the hospice CEO. A couple of weeks before the meeting, he had asked each of us to review several documents outlining our financial data, our patient care data, and a gaggle of graphs containing mind-numbing information that meant nothing to me. I was the director of quality service, and while I *was* a senior manager, the higher-level organizational data was not something that I was routinely involved in. So I took a cursory review of the numbers, jotted a few notes to look as though I'd studied them, and stuck the paperwork in my folder for the meeting.

The CEO began the meeting by saying, "I'd like to hear your interpretations of the data I sent you."

As one of the least important people in the room and feeling much less responsible for the data than the others, I sat quietly and watched to see what the more experienced leaders would say.

They didn't say anything.

I don't mean they rambled on in incoherent circuitous analysis that didn't make sense. I mean, they didn't say *anything*.

The CEO said, "Did you read this?"

A few people said, "Yes." But there answers weren't very convincing.

"Then what do you think?"

Our PR person, who was very good in these situations, said, "Well, there are a lot of ways we could interpret the information."

Just a tip. Never use the we-could-interpret-it-in-many-ways response. It's a clear sign that we don't know what we're talking about but that we don't have the guts to admit it.

The CEO turned a unfamiliar shade of red, stood up, and said, "I am very disappointed that none of you felt this information was important enough to read. Clearly, you don't respect the work enough to do it correctly." He went on, "I'm leaving for vacation today and for the next two weeks, I'm going to give this some thought. When I return, things are going to change."

We sat there stunned. He had never acted like this and we had never felt so irresponsible. Thank goodness we wouldn't have to deal with him again for two weeks. Par-tee!

I once read the results of a study indicating that 85% of people surveyed said they hated meetings. I think most people would rather work on their own projects, or their own appendectomy for that matter, rather than to be cooped up in a room, engaged in endless discussions that accomplish nothing—because that's how a many meetings work.

In my example above, our CEO was ultimately responsible for the outcome of meeting, and his responsibility not only started before the meeting began but continued after the meeting ended. And yet we also had responsibility for the outcome of the meeting. And therein lies the problem. Most people, whether the leaders or the participants, don't take responsibility for the meeting itself. They may or may not do the necessary work outside of the meeting, but they don't usually consider the process of participating in the meeting as part of that work. And yet, there are some very simple steps that anyone can take to make meetings better.

Meetings Minus Mundane Means M-Proved

Meetings are a necessary evil in the work environment, and we must accept that there will always be some sort of gathering to discuss the workings of the organization whether live, via conference call, or by video. The problem is that most people just succumb to the evil of meetings and never consider how to make the experience both more effective and more fun. While it *is* a skill to run a meeting, it's not rocket surgery and can be easily learned by anyone.

I was responsible for running quality improvement meetings when I worked in hospice, and if I must be candid, the meetings were awful. After the second of these meetings, people threatened to skip the future meetings because they didn't find them helpful. Not only was the content boring, but a number of participants really didn't want to be there. So I had a challenge in front of me. Feeling a bit desperate at the end of the second meeting, I made a promise to everyone that if they came back to the third meeting, the experience would be different. I had to come up with some way to make the meetings more effective *and* enjoyable.

At each meeting, I was responsible for giving a verbal report of all the quality projects that were going on throughout the organization. This was just a boring rundown of projects, statistics, and outcomes. Most people brought sleeping bags for this portion of the meeting. But at the third meeting, I surprised them. Instead of charts and graphs, I sang my report. Yes, I sang my report to the tune of the *Gilligan's Island* theme song. People sat up, laughed, and started humming along. It totally changed the atmosphere of the meeting.

And the funny thing was, we not only finished 15 minutes early, we accomplished more than the previous two meeting combined. At subsequent meetings, we had competitions to guess the data in my report, I gave out prizes, and we had a much more enjoyable meeting experience.

The Well-Fun-Meeting Process

If our job requires that we be a part of a team, committee, or project, we will have to be in meetings. Let's look at a few simple tips for running an effective meeting.

Do It Well

1. **The person running the meeting is a facilitator, not a leader, not a lobbyist, and certainly not a dictator.** The best meetings are the ones that run effectively and efficiently and we don't even realize that the person in charge has done anything. Facilitation means guiding the process and helping the participants move toward the desired outcomes. It's not about forcing—but more like nudging. In meetings, the process is very important.

2. **The agenda is a tool and should be used.** It lets participants know what to expect and it allows the facilitator to move the meeting along. The agenda should be sent out to all participants prior to the meeting (a week is suggested) and all agenda items should have timelines associated with them so that each participant knows how much time is allotted for the discussion. Then, anyone who goes over the allotted time must either conclude the discussion or buy back time from someone else's item on the agenda so that the meeting ends as scheduled. Don't just discuss

things until the wee hours of the night. One of the most important agenda items that should be listed after every item on the agenda is this: What the heck is going to happen and who the heck is responsible for it? This is a way of assuring that the outcome of the discussion item actually gets accomplished.

3. **This thing called minutes, which is really a document that captures hours of discussions, is another critical element of the meeting process.** Minutes, or an overview of the discussions and decisions, should be completed within 72 hours of the meeting and distributed to participants while the information is still fresh in their minds. Otherwise, participants will not remember the specifics and only glance at it. Participants should read minutes both for accuracy and to remind them of their responsibilities for the next meeting.

Make It Fun

1. **Make meeting management fun.** Assign an enforcer to make sure ground rules are adhered to or to call time when someone talks too much. Label the agenda items with funny labels such as "Bored Meeting" instead of "Board Meeting." Jazz up reports with funny slides, songs, or skits to keep participants engaged. Change the meeting location to a restaurant or coffee shop.

2. **Make the minutes of the meeting fun to read.** Hide a joke or use play on words to report on the discussions. Give a prize to the first person to find the joke.

3. **Make discussions fun.** Instead of just seeking input, consider games and competitions to draw out the best ideas.

Then, keep members engaged by regularly rewarding them with fun gifts (candy, gum,etc.) whenever they participate.

If we make meetings work well, they will work well for us. And if we make them fun, people won't hate them so much.

Chapter 20

Unlike a Steak, a Project Well Done Is Rare

My worst car-buying experience happened when we were buying a replacement car for Wendy. We had done some research and at the time, the Honda Accord was one of the best rated cars on the market. So we went to a Honda dealer in Tysons Corner, Virginia, to purchase one. We were walking around the lot when a salesman approached us and asked if he could help. Hesitantly, because he was a car salesman, we agreed.

He showed us several cars and we decided to test drive the one we liked. We really liked it, the price was right, and we were prepared to buy one that day. So we told the salesman we wanted to buy the car. Then, everything changed. We now entered the phase of the buying experience called The Negotiation Process, or as we refer to it, the Lose-All-of-Your-Dignity-By-Dickering-Over-Every-Penny Process. But before the actual process started, the salesman said he needed to take our current car into the shop to assess the trade-in value. He took my keys and I watched my car disappear into one of the service bays in the back. I didn't feel good about that.

The salesman then escorted us over to an empty desk with a dummy phone and one paper clip on it, and had us sit in comfortable chairs while he took out a sheet of paper specifically designed for negotiating. He said to me, "How would you feel about car payments of $299 per month?"

I said, "For how long?"

He said, "I don't know."

I said, "Then I don't feel too good about it."

He scratched out the $299 and began writing on the negotiation sheet. First, he listed the so-called real value of the car, which was much higher than the number on the sticker. Then he subtracted several numbers, which he claimed were "today-only" discounts. Finally, he arrived at a number that looked amazingly similar to the original sticker price and said, "The car costs $21,999, but I can let you drive it home today for $21,998. That's a great bargain for this car, the most popular car in the northern hemisphere."

We explained that we had done research on the car and, based on everything we read, we should be able to buy it for $18,999—and we weren't going to pay more than that. Apparently, this salesman wasn't familiar with the word "weren't." He said that price was impossible . . . (dramatic pause) . . . but he would speak to his manager and "see what I can do."

He came back and offered us $21,997 as "the lowest he would be able to go."

We explained that we were prepared to pay $18,999 and that we were not (we avoided the contraction this time) going to pay more than that. He said he was pretty sure it was an impossible number but he would speak to his manager. A few minutes later, he came back and offered us a "surprising price—because my manager is feeling generous."

He said we could drive the car off the lot today for $21,900 but no less.

I began to grind my teeth.

This went on for two and a half hours until I finally said that I was tired of this process and besides, the salesman was wearing out the carpet between his desk and the manager's office. I stood up and headed for the door when I realized that I didn't have the keys to my own car. It was still in the service bay being appraised. I turned around to tell the salesman that I wanted my car. He was walking toward me, this time with the manager. Uh-oh.

The manager said that he was willing to meet my price but not before he told me that he was making no money from the sale and that by lowering the price on this car, *we* would be putting *him* out of business and keeping his children from going to college. I think I even saw a tear in the corner of his eye.

I looked at my Wendy, then back at the manager, and then said, "I'm sorry, but we're no longer interested. Please bring me my car and we'll be on our way."

Both the salesman, the manager, *and* Wendy were stunned. Clearly this had never happened to them.

"But we met your price," the manager said.

"Yeah, but it took you two and a half hours to do it. You made it extremely difficult on me. And I don't want to give you my business. I'm a sore winner."

By then, my car had been brought around and I had my keys. I walked confidently to the car, and just before I got in, Wendy grabbed my arm and said, "They met our price. *Why* are you leaving?"

"Because they put us through too much grief to get to our price. It's taken us almost three hours."

She said, "Yes, but now, we'll have to go somewhere else and go through the whole thing again. Are you nuts?"

She had a point. The "whole thing" part, not the "nuts" part.

I looked at her. I looked at the dealer. I looked toward the ground, knowing I would have to relent. There was no easy way to back down.

So I marched back into the store and said, "You're lucky that my wife feels sorry for you. I'll buy your stupid car."

My wife never bought a Honda again. Don't tell her, but I did. I just told her it was a Hyundai. It's amazing what I can do with a black permanent marker.

The problem with buying a car, other than the fact that nobody knows what the real numbers are, is that the process is broken. It's an ineffective process designed to benefit only the dealer, and it's a bad process for the customer. So we can't manage it well. But processes are not that hard to manage.

Turning a Process and a Project Around

About ten years ago, I agreed to represent my Rotary Club on the Monte Carlo Night fund-raiser planning committee. Monte Carlo Night was an event cosponsored by five Rotary Clubs that involved food, music, a casino, a silent auction, and a live auction. The event attracted nearly 400 participants and raised over $65,000. It was one of the largest fund-raisers for our club.

But the Monte Carlo Night planning process was very poorly organized.

Representatives from each of the Rotary Clubs would meet, starting about five months in advance, to plan all the details of the event, from contracting with the casino operators to selecting the menu from the hotel. At my first meeting, the most common question I heard was, "How did we do this last year?"

There were no written policies, no procedures, and no guidelines. We were flying by the seat of our pants and surprisingly, the event was still successful.

One guy who had been involved in chairing the committee for several years was the corporate memory for the event. If he left (which he did two years later), we would have been in sad shape. So my contribution to the planning committee was to organize a procedural manual so we wouldn't have to reinvent the blessed wheel every year thereafter.

And that's my philosophy about managing processes and projects. There are steps to every process, and if we break them down and record them, we'll have a nice little step-by-step guide to completion. Most people, however, would rather fly by the seat of their Brooks Brothers and just adjust if they run into trouble. That style of project management not only drives the project team crazy, it will likely create more work for everyone involved.

The Well-Fun-Project Process

The following are tips for running processes and projects. It's simple but effective. After running through the steps, I'll show you how to make it more fun.

Do It Well

1. **Create the team and the timeline**. Before the project begins, the chairperson must select a capable group of people to assist with the project. Please note that the word *capable* means people who not only have the necessary expertise but will also do the work. A lot of smart people who would love to show up at a meeting and impress people with their knowledge will have no interest in helping with any of the tasks and are not capable team members. These people are deadwood and should be left to drift rather than weighing the project down.

2. **Engage the participants and create buy-in for the project**. Convene the first meeting with the capable people from the

first step. This is the beginning of both the project and the team building that must occur to get the work done. Take time to go over the background information, explaining why the project was developed, why the work must be done, and why this group of participants is the group to do it. You must connect the dots that might be obvious to you and then create excitement about the project.

3. **Manage the process**. If you read the chapter on managing meetings, process or project management is very similar. The goal of the chairperson is to manage all the parts of the process to get to the goal. At each meeting, there must be a report on the work done since the last meeting. Then the group must assess the effectiveness of the work done, make the necessary adjustments, and then identify the tasks to be done next. As the project progresses, write everything down so the next group will know what to do.

Make It Fun

1. In order to make the progress of the work more enjoyable and to **continue to engage the group members, create fun, interesting, or intriguing benchmarks for the work**. Benchmarks are measurable goals that align with progress toward the overall goal. For instance, if planning a fundraiser with a casino, at some point, the casino company must be engaged, a contract negotiated, and a deposit paid. Fun benchmarks make the hitting of the goals more fun and can include tote boards with bells and whistles, announcements to colleagues about progress, skits, musical performance explaining progress, or other such extravaganzas. For example, one hospital's quality improvement effort was highlighted every few months with funny videos shared throughout the hospital's internal television station.

2. **Reward and acknowledge the participants**. At each meeting, as you report on work done since the previous meeting, make necessary adjustments, identify the tasks on the schedule to be done next, and recognize the members of the committee and the progress made thus far. It doesn't matter if the participants are staff or volunteers; people appreciate being appreciated. Consider using fun methods to recognize the work such as gag gifs, gift certificates, or simply clever public recognitions. For example, one organization presented a framed photo of a staff member (yours truly) in drag to a member of the team who did something creative. The photo became an icon of creative thinking and the individual got to keep the photo in his/her office until it was given to someone else.

3. **Celebrate the achievement of the committee**—regardless of the outcome. At the final meeting of the team, you have either succeeded in your goal or failed miserably. Review the results of the project and the process. Take careful notes about those things that worked well and those that didn't. And remember, our egos will want to relinquish responsibility for any failures. However, growth and future success depend on a valid assessment of the process. After you've made an accurate assessment of the work that was done, celebrate like it is 1999. Celebrate the teamwork, the time, the energy, and the effort contributed by the team. That's always worth something. You can even have this meeting off-site where you can share pizza, drinks, or a happy meal together as you celebrate.

When I worked in quality improvement, I read a great story of a regulatory group that was interviewing a janitor at one of NASA's facilities. The interviewer asked the janitor, "What do you do here?"

The janitor said, "I help put people on the moon."

If all project team members, or all employees, for that matter, saw the importance of their work relative to the overall mission of the organization, every project would be done with excellence.

Every process has steps. By paying attention to the steps, we can manage the process better. And while it might be rare, if we do it right, the project will be well done and fun.

Chapter 21

Bored to Death

All work and no play makes Jack a dull boy, a boring conversationalist, and burnt out at the age of 50.

Have you ever attended a social gathering and the person next to you talks incessantly about their work? It's horrible. Especially if their work involves something we know nothing about—like calibrating thermodynamic thrust capacitors for low-resistance cog twirlers. These people are so caught up in their work, they can't talk about anything else—even the weather.

Me: "Wow, it's been really hot this week."

Them: "Affirmative. The heat plays havoc with our capacitors causing the calibrators to leap off the flaxo dial. I thought I'd have to pull some extra hours this week just to figure out the metrics. It's crazy."

People like this need a hobby. While I admire their investment in their work, work *is* not and *should* not be everything in our lives. That's what hobbies are for. Balance. Recreation. Relaxation. A break from work. But you'd be amazed at how many people have no hobbies.

My dad didn't have any real hobbies. Oh, he puttered (what old people do) in the yard, pulling up weeds and picking up sticks. And for a few years, he made miniature bird houses as Christmas ornaments. This was very fun for him until his hand-to-eye coordination made it more frustrating than rewarding. But as he got older, we used to kid him that his true hobby was sitting in a chair all day just waiting to go to bed that night. It was more truthful than we'd like to admit. And it saddens me that he didn't have more things to keep him busy between the time he retired and when he died. Eventually, he did discover the History Channel and that was fun for him.

My mom, on the other hand, can't keep up with all of her hobbies. She knits, crochets, goes out to eat, calls her friends, reads books, goes out to eat, plays bridge, and is a member of several clubs. One of them is called the Half Century Club. My mom is 89. It should be called the Three-Quarter+ Century Club. But the point is that I believe my mom stays young and vibrant because of her hobbies. If it wasn't for that, she'd have nothing to do but sit around thinking about how bored she is. And we all know older people who do just that.

I've always been a jack-of-all-trades. In other words, I've been reasonably good at a lot of things rather than being incredibly good at a few things. In high school, I played in the band, played tennis and basketball, ran track, performed in a play, and wrote humor for special events. In college, I was in a service fraternity, played intramural basketball, played in the band, volunteered with a youth basketball league, and was a semiprofessional beer drinker. While I wasn't a straight-A student, I can't help but believe that my average, yet well-rounded, experience was a long-term benefit. And in the spirit of full disclosure, I also did cross-stitch. Yep. I learned to do cross-stitch in my high school art class. It came in handy when I worked night shifts at the psychiatric hospital because it was the only thing I could do without falling asleep. It's not the most manly of hobbies, but it's relaxing and gives me a sense of creative accomplishment. Just the same, I'd prefer that you not tell anyone about that.

Early in my career, a colleague suggested that I do fun things when my business was slow because, as it got busier, I wouldn't have time for the fun stuff. So when things were slow, I played golf, rode my motorcycle, or read a novel. Then, when it got busy, I didn't feel as if I never had time to enjoy my hobbies.

Today, I read, I ride my motorcycle, I mountain bike, and I play golf. Oh, and I bought a cross-stitch project that's so big, it will take me until I'm 200 years old to finish. But it's something to shoot for.

Do you have hobbies? If not, why? Do you consider your work so much fun that you don't need a hobby? If so, you're on the path to burnout and a friendless existence. A rich life is about balance. And balance is about mixing work and play, the good and the bad, the lemon and the lime. It's about expanding our horizons by experiencing new things. That's where doing it well and making it fun really resonates.

And, for the record, television, video games, and computer solitaire are not really hobbies. They're distracting and fun, but in the long run they don't really provide us with any long-term benefit. If, on the other hand, we watch movies with our spouse as a hobby or we're involved in competitive online games in which we win money or prizes, that's more likely a hobby.

Am I Too Old for This?

There used to be a show on MTV called *Scarred* that was packed with videos of young thrill-seekers who break bones, crack skulls, and crush their "egos" while engaging in extreme skateboarding, bicycling, and other dangerous "ing" activities. I secretly loved that show! While the twisted body parts pushed my fainting threshold to the test, I think the crashes stimulated some sort of testosterone-laden, midlife, agony-of-defeat gland in my head that released a pleasant surge of serotonin throughout my body.

Now, I'm no risk junkie, but I do believe my desire for risk has increased as I have approached midlife (OK, fine, so I'm already there). It's as if I know that one day, when I'm playing balloon tennis in an assisted-living facility, I'll wish I had taken more risks. And I don't think I'm alone. Many middle-aged men seek the risk of a woman half their age or a convertible that's one speeding ticket away from a suspended license. And aging women seek the risk of a Botox needle or stretching the limit on their credit cards.

For me the rush comes from athletic activities that are well beyond my physical and mental abilities. For instance, a few years ago, I started snowboarding because I could never get the hang of skiing. Turns out, I don't seem to have the hang of snowboarding, either. My son and I also bought mountain bikes, since road biking was boring to us. Before we went out the first time, we sought the council of my younger, physically fitter neighbor Gill, who is an excellent mountain biker.

In the parking lot next to the course, Gill suggested that we go over a few important "techniques" before we hit the trail. I watched him demonstrate the proper braking, leaning, and steering maneuvers and then I saw him "jump" his bike over small curb. The maneuver looked relatively simple and, being the confident student that I am, I gave it a shot.

I yanked on the handlebars so that my front wheel lifted a full 2 millimeters off the ground. The back wheel stayed glued to the pavement. The weight of my body forced my right foot off the pedal, and as my foot slammed to the ground, the pedal ripped across my shin. Blood ran down my leg. It really hurt and yet the adrenaline pumped through my veins like a shot of espresso. I was now ready for the rugged trail, especially since it's in the woods and quite a bit darker, so that no one would see that I had hurt myself while still in the parking lot.

The course was tough, but we took it easy until we got our trail legs, so to speak. It was fun and the feeling of riding downhill over roots and rocks was quite a rush. The next week, I returned to the same course with more confidence and less fear. At one creek crossing, I tried to pop my front wheel onto a small slat bridge. Somehow the wheel became jammed against the first slat and the ground. Regrettably, my front brake was fully engaged, which, according to some obscure law of physics, locked my front wheel, causing my back wheel to rise up in the air like a cheap carnival ride, taking me over the handlebars toward the bridge and the creek. Being the agile, deceptively young-minded stud that I am, I avoided a nasty crash by jumping off the bike. Luckily no one was looking, but a brush with a broken collarbone led to another rush of adrenaline. It was better than Red Bull with a Mountain Dew chaser.

The next week I rode the trail by myself. Wendy casually asked what I'd do if I crashed while on the course alone. I assured her that I had my cell phone with me and as long as I was physically able to use it, I'd call for help. She just shook her head and called our insurance carrier to see if stupidity was covered under our policy.

My ride was going well until I got to that same slat bridge that had given me trouble the week before. Confident in my improved skills, I knew I could tackle it this time. Apparently, however, there is a part of the brain that remembers past traumas and will do everything within its power to prevent us from reliving them. This cranial alert system sends signals throughout the body, leading to significantly diminished physical reaction times. As a result of this mind-body phenomenon, I once again took flight over my handlebars. This time, however, my foot was stuck to the pedal and I sailed over the bridge into the embankment on the other side of the creek.

I was covered in mud, the bike was on top of me, and my shoulder was buried in the ground. Nothing on me or the bike was broken, and luckily no one saw me fall. But the adrenaline rush was overwhelming. Two days later, my thighs looked like a purple mountain majesty. I was scarred for midlife.

My mountain biking was a bit dangerous. But most hobbies should entertain, expand our mind, and help us improve upon a particular skill.

The Well-Fun-Hobby Process

So, here are my simple steps to embracing a hobby so that you don't go to the grave as a perpetual employee. Since hobbies are supposed to be fun, you get one list with six items this time around.

Do It Well *and* Make It Fun.

1. **Make a bucket list** of all the things you'd like to do before you die. If the list is extensive, it might allow you to do a variety of things as your hobby rather than focusing on one or two. The list, however, this is a good starting point for developing your work-life balance plan.

2. Many of us have a sport in which we always wanted to participate. If physically able, **look for local groups that may offer an opportunity to join a team**. Fifty-year-olds should probably not participate in full-contact tackle football, but we're not necessarily ready for balloon tennis either. I'm just saying.

3. If you enjoy reading, you can **join a book club**. By becoming a member of a club, you're forced to read at least one book a month. And being forced to pursue a hobby is not a bad thing.

4. If crafts like cross-stitch are your thing, **local community centers and libraries offer classes to learn a variety of crafts** and to practice them with other enthusiasts. There's

nothing better than a little bonding with another male cross-stitcher.

5. **The Internet is a great tool for finding people who have the same interests that you have.** There are groups within Facebook and Twitter that allow you to connect with others to share ideas about a lot of different hobbies.

6. Finally, **engage in your hobby at least once per week.** If you don't schedule it, you'll neglect it. If you neglect it, you don't reap the benefits.

Work is not a hobby. Hobbies should not be work. But blending work with hobbies is nirvana and the essence of doing it well and making it fun.

Chapter 22

Donating Our Time for Fun and Profit

A few years ago, I was a bit overextended. I served on the governing board of my church and was also chairing several committees that needed some help getting back on track. On top of that, I was president of the local chapter of the National Speakers Association, a member of my local Rotary club (responsible for two of our largest fund-raisers), and on a committee for my son's Boy Scout troop. Did I mention that I was also running my own business as a full-time speaker and author?

It was during my overwhelmedness that I realized I had been volunteering too much. Well, that's not exactly right. I wasn't volunteering too much. I was volunteering for too many large, time-consuming projects. I was getting burned out and beginning to resent my volunteer responsibilities.

A year after I finished doing time, that is, serving on my church's governing board, Gerri, a member of the nominating committee, called me to see if I would consider serving on the church's board of trustees. The trustees were the bean counters who were mostly concerned with the cost of a replacement for the kitchen fan or the mileage that the church van got. That was not my cup of tea. So, I very calmly told Gerri, "Put the phone down, step slowly away, and no one will get hurt."

I was not about to submit myself to a hectic volunteer schedule again, especially on a committee I didn't enjoy.

But here's the problem. I was a living example of the Pareto principle. Named after Italian economist Vilfredo Pareto, this principle states that 80% of the effects of something are due to 20% of the causes. When it comes to volunteering, this principle suggests that 80% of the work is done by 20% of the volunteers. I have been part of that 20% many times. In my church. In my Rotary club. And currently in my professional association. However, without this core of volunteers, many nonprofit organizations would never get the work done.

I believe in volunteerism. I believe in grassroots organizing. And I believe that more people should commit their time, energy, and financial resources to volunteer efforts. I know that I am richer because of what I give. The old saying that it's better to give than to receive is true. Especially if you give away a really bad gift that you received.

I think we would all be better if we focused more on what we can do for others rather than what others can do for us. And I'm one of the most self-centered narcissists you'll ever meet. Is that redundant?

It's a Matter of Reframing

About seven years ago, I was frustrated with the way my volunteer activities kept interfering with my work. Art Berg, a speaker colleague whom I never had the privilege of meeting, once said that one of his children interrupted him one day while he was working. He was frustrated because he felt his kids were often interrupting him. Then, it occurred to him that, in reality, his work was interrupting his family. This was an important insight and made a big impact on me.

I realized that my volunteer activities didn't have to interfere with my work—especially if I reframed the situation and viewed them as *part* of my work. So I changed my business model. I included volunteering as part of the mission of my business. Oh sure, I want to have a profitable business while using my gifts and skills to provide something of value to others. But I also consider my mission to include volunteering. By reframing the situation, I don't resent those weeks when my volunteer activities take on a little more time than usual, any more than I would when my work activities take more time than usual.

Today, I commit about one quarter of my time to volunteering and community service. I don't tell you this to brag or to act as if I somehow have more integrity than anyone else, even though I certainly might. I tell you this because I'd love to see you consider the same adjustment to your work and volunteer balance: to look at volunteering as part of what we do rather than something we add on *when* we have the time.

We need more volunteers. The effects of the economy have hit nonprofit organizations hard. Many cannot offer the services they once did. However, volunteers can help get them back in the black to continue their mission.

The Personal Benefits of Volunteering

As a volunteer emcee for the Herndon Chamber of Commerce's annual awards banquet, I had the privilege of participating in a historic event. The awards banquet occurred during the 400th anniversary of the founding of the State of Virginia, so every former governor of Virginia had been invited to attend the event. Three showed up: Doug Wilder, the first African-American governor in the country; George Allen, former U.S. senator who had just been unseated; and James Gilmore who, at the time, was running for president of the United States (it was a very short campaign, unfortunately). As emcee, I was seated at their table and spent the evening hearing stories of politics and chatting with these fantastic leaders.

All three former governors spoke, and in each case, I listened very carefully so that I could use their comments to segue to the next speaker as well as to make fun of them in any politically correct way I could. Doug Wilder gave the most compelling speech. He was part politician and part Baptist minister. He had the crowd worked up, and they leapt to their feet when he finished. I was very inspired. One of his most poignant comments was when he said that as a child he had read the Declaration of Independence and saw that "all men are created equal." He said he felt that Thomas Jefferson was speaking directly to him and that he could accomplish anything he wanted. For an African-American growing up when and where he did, this was quite inspiring.

After Governor Wilder left the stage, I returned to my emcee role to introduce the next part of the program. I said, "As a graduate of the University of Virginia, which was founded by Thomas Jefferson, I too had many experiences in college when I felt that Thomas Jefferson was speaking directly to me. It was only a few years after I graduated that I realized that, in each case, it was the tequila talking."

I saw Doug Wilder double over in laughter and punch George Allen in the arm. It was one of my greatest moments as a speaker, an emcee, and as a volunteer.

The Well-Fun-Volunteer Process

So, how can we help the cause by becoming a more active volunteer? Consider these few guidelines.

Do It Well

1. If you **find a cause in which you believe**, volunteering is more meaningful. Perhaps it's your church or synagogue—that is, if you believe enough! Maybe it's a free

clinic in your town. Or maybe it's the Rotary Club's fight to eliminate polio. Whatever it is, you should find something nearby that floats your boat.

2. **Determine how your gifts, skills, and financial resources** can help this effort. I'm a speaker so I often emcee fundraisers and awards dinners as a way to contribute my skills. I've also donated free stress-management programs for the teachers in my kids' schools. Maybe you have computer skills or you're really good at organizing. Whatever it is, we all can offer what we're good at.

3. **Promote these volunteer organizations to others**. I always talk about Rotary, the National Speakers Association, my church, our free clinic, and other groups in which I'm involved. It allows me to promote the good work they're doing as well as to encourage others to volunteer.

Make It Fun

1. **Always volunteer with a fun spirit**. The great thing about volunteering is that we're volunteers. It's not a job, so we should not feel locked into being overly serious. By having a fun spirit, we become role models and encourage others to volunteer as well.

2. **Find the fun jobs to volunteer for**. When I worked for the Jeanne Schmidt Free Clinic, I helped clean up after the clinic closed. It was easy and fun, and it satisfied my OCD-ness. Even though I was a social worker, I didn't want to be that during my evenings. So this was more fun for me.

3. **If you feel yourself being drained emotionally and physically by volunteering, either quit, take a break, or find**

another organization in which to volunteer. There is nothing worse than a grumpy volunteer.

Volunteering is about giving of ourselves. But if we're giving in a way that's helpful to others and fun to us, it gives back.

Chapter 23

When All Is Said and Done

We've come to the end of the book, and it's here that I'm supposed to wrap everything up with a poem, a heart-wrenching story, or a surprise ending that makes you put the book down thinking that you'll never read another book that affected you the way this one did. If that's what you're looking for, I'm afraid I might just disappoint you.

You see, there is nothing poetic, heart-wrenching, surprising, or particularly profound about Do It Well, Make It Fun. It's simple, really. We have a limited time on the planet, and during that time, we have many choices to make about how we live our lives. We can cruise on autopilot or we can take a little extra time and energy and focus on excellence and joy.

My hope is that this book made you think. And that it made you laugh. And most importantly, that it will encourage you to change your lifestyle, so that when you get to the end of your life you will look back and say that it was "well done . . . and fun."

Good luck.